Tales of Our Youth

Generations of Love & Hope

by

Elizabeth Brown

Rose Anne
My best wishes to you.
I hope you enjoy reading
this book
Elizabeth Brown

Brighton Publishing LLC
501 W. Ray Road
Suite 4
Chandler, AZ 85225

Tales of Our Youth
Generations of Love & Hope

by

Elizabeth Brown

Published by
Brighton Publishing LLC
501 W. Ray Road
Suite 4
Chandler, AZ 85225
www.BrightonPublishing.com

Copyright © 2012

ISBN 13: 978-1-621830-34-4
ISBN 10: 1-62183034-9

Printed in the United States of America

First Edition

Cover Design by Tom Rodriguez
Painting depicted on cover painted by Billie Mallough

Our life on the farm

Back through the years
We go wandering once again
Back to the seasons of our youth

Alois Pierzina Family

1963

Back row – Dwaine, Bette, Dianne, Judy, Russell
Front row – Father Alois, George, Mother Helen

❧ *Dedication* ❧

I dedicate this book to you the reader in the hope that it rekindles a forgotten memory you had tucked away and you can relive some of the joys from your own childhood. And to our children, grandchildren, and future generations to come.

❧ Acknowledgements ❦

Many thanks to my sisters and brothers for their treasured memories and their help; especially Dwaine, who could answer any question I threw at him.

≈ Creation of Mother ≈

When the Good Lord was creating Mother he was into his sixth day of "overtime" when the angel appeared and said, "You're doing a lot of fiddling around on this one."

And the Lord said, "Have you read the specs on this order? She has to be completely washable, but not plastic. Have 180 moveable parts...all replaceable. Run on black coffee and leftovers. Have a lap that disappears when she stands up. A kiss that can cure anything from a broken leg to a disappointed love affair. And six pairs of hands."

The angel shook her head slowly and said, "Six pairs of hands...no way."

It's not the hands that are causing me problems," said the Lord, "It's the three pairs of eyes that Mothers have to have."

"That's on the standard model?" asked the angel.

The Lord nodded. "One pair that sees through closed doors when she asks, 'What are you kids doing in there?' when she already knows. Another here in the back of her head that sees what she shouldn't but what she has to know, and of course the ones here in front that can look at a child when he goofs up and say, 'I understand and I love you' without so much as uttering a word."

"Lord," said the angel touching His sleeve gently, "Come to bed. Tomorrow..."

"I can't," said the Lord, "I'm so close to creating something so close to myself. Already I have one who heals herself when she is sick...can feed a family of eight on one pound of hamburger...and can get a nine-year-old to stand under a shower."

The angel circled the model of a Mother very slowly. "It's too soft," she sighed.

"But tough!" said the Lord excitedly. "You cannot imagine what this Mother can do or endure."

"Can it think?"

"Not only think, but it can reason and compromise," said the Creator.

Finally the angel bent over and ran her finger across the cheek. "There's a leak," she pronounced. "I told you, you were trying to put too much into this model."

"It's not a leak," said the Lord, "it's a tear."

"What's it for?"

"It's for joy, sadness, disappointment, pain, loneliness and pride."

"You are a genius," said the angel.

The Lord looked somber. "I didn't put it there."

Erma Bombeck

❧ Chapter One ❦

Swan River Farm

O ur father Alois Pierzina was born in Bowlus, Minnesota on February 4, 1912. His parents were George and Louise (Blair) Pierzina. He was the second born of eight children. He spent his early years in the town of Bowlus where his father George was a very industrious man. Among some of his credits, he operated the New Grand Hotel, which was owned by his father John Pierzina. George was town Marshall, member of City Council, member of the School Board, member of Highway Layout. He also owned Bowlus Implement Company, which carried machinery and supplies for the farmers, and a Feed Mill where the local farmers brought their grain and corn to be ground.

In January, 1920 Prohibition was signed into law prohibiting the sale of alcohol. When the men could no longer buy their spirits they began to make it themselves. They designed and built what was called a "still" which was usually hidden deep in the woods away from public view and the law. The alcohol was called "Moonshine." Moonshine was made from any product they could find, including lye and many other highly dangerous ingredients. George and his friends were involved in the moonshine business and also their own destruction. His very prosperous business also started a downward spiral.

When our dad, Alois, was eleven years old, they lost their home. It was December 23, 1923 when Louise's father, Peter Blair, took his wife Emma to the train depot where she was going to spend a couple of months visiting the west coast and Texas. Afterward he stopped by to visit his daughter and found them in dire straits. She was now pregnant with her seventh child and a bleak future. He gathered up the six children and Louise and took them all home with him.

George lost his businesses, his home, and his family. The children finished growing up on the Blair farm and our dad remained there until he married our mom. George was always welcome to come and visit his family, but when Louise became pregnant with her eighth child, the welcome mat was removed. A few years later Louise divorced George. The Peter Blair farm was located in the general Bowlus area but was called Swan River Township. Townships were rural farming areas, each area was given a name identifying them, but they were not actual towns

A frequent visitor to the Blair farm was Charles A. Lindberg of aviator fame, first to fly across the Atlantic to France. The Mississippi River runs through the center of Little Falls, dividing the city in half. He lived on the west side of town on the banks of the river. His home was located between the town of Little Falls and the Blair's, and he always enjoyed taking part in the chores and harvesting. He did this while he was still a teenager but he left the area before our dad and family moved onto the Blair farm.

Our mother was Helen Gertrude Hankes, and was better known by friends and family as Girlie. She was born on December 7, 1920 in Tripoli, Wisconsin. Her parents were Frank and Ella (Robinson) Hankes, both born and raised in St. Cloud, Minnesota. After their marriage, they moved to St. Paul where Frank worked in a cigar making factory, which he had done since he was six years old in St. Cloud. Then they decided to take up farming and moved to Tripoli, Wisconsin shortly before the birth of our mother. She was the fourth child of six. When she was a little girl she was sitting by the side of the road and a car came by and the lady in the car said, "Hello Girlie". Mom went in the house and told her parents what the lady called her and for some reason the name stuck.

While living in Wisconsin, Prohibition was also the law of the land, and Grandpa Frank—along with farming—was in the moonshine business, too but he was able to outsmart the Feds. The Feds were from the Federal government law enforcement. They would invade and break up the stills and confiscate the liquor. The Feds knew that Grandpa was moonshining but were unable to find a stash on his farm. Years later, one of the officers asked him how he was able to elude them and Grandpa told him that his agents were always very careful where they stepped. Grandpa covered his tracks well. After the cows went to the bathroom; the remains were called a cow pie, which would dry in the sun and harden into a flat object, similar to a plate but larger. Grandpa would dig a hole in the ground, hollow it out, and place his moonshine inside the hole and place the dry manure over the top. The agents being careful where they stepped never discovered his secret so he was never caught. Grandpa always got a big chuckle when retelling this story.

The difference between the two grandfathers and how they operated their side businesses was that Grandpa Frank made moonshine and sold it generating some extra cash but Grandpa George made it and consumed it.

In 1930 when Mom was ten years old, they decided to move to North Dakota. Being from the St. Cloud area originally, they visited with family and friends there. They ended up thirty miles north in Little Falls and Frank gained employment through WPA, (government work program) at Camp Ripley. They bought acreage in Green Prairie Township where Frank, with only a hammer and a saw, built the home that still stands today.

They moved there in October and sadly their oldest son Elmer at age nineteen drowned in the Mississippi River eight months later. The river was located about a mile from their home. He was spearing for fish and caught a knapsack full when he stepped in a hole that the ever-changing swift current created. He was a good, strong swimmer, but the heavy knapsack and waders prevented him from reaching shore. He was observed struggling, but help was unable to reach him in time.

Both of our parents were loved and enjoyed by all who knew them, having easy going personalities and quick to laugh and enjoy a good time. Neither of them was grumpy or overly stern. Mother would go-with-the-flow but father would dig his heels in and could not be budged. Years later we realized she also had a bit of a stubborn streak.

Mom was slender and tall, standing 5' 8" and weighed about 105 pounds. She had light brown hair, green eyes, and a pretty face. Her maternal grandfather was Scotch Irish; a long lineage of relatives lived in Maine. Her other grandparents emigrated from Sweden, Luxemburg and Germany.

Daddy was 5'11" and weighed about 175 pounds. Although he was lean, he was not of a bony structure. He had dark-brown eyes and black hair. Being of Polish, German, and French descent, the French was most prominent. All of his grandparents were immigrants and spoke their native tongues: Polish, German and French. As children, they had to be able to understand each of the languages to communicate with them, and they did. The men adapted well to the English language but the women spoke their native tongue.

Alois with his mother Louise

He went to work in Iowa with a threshing crew and bought her this dress. She just loved it.

Our dad had many fine qualities and was admired by all who knew him. He was confident, charismatic, hardworking, highly respected, very high morals, and very protective of his family. He was not impulsive and gave a lot of thought and planned things through carefully, always making the right choice.

He believed that if you take on a job, whether it's building a building or doing a repair job, do it the right way the first time, then you won't have to go back and do it over again in the future. It was also important to take care of what you have; and if maintained properly, it should last a lifetime.

They say that his father George had the ability to add a column of figures in his head without paper and it seems that our dad got some of that gift from him. He was good at math and an

5

excellent record keeper. Not only was he farming for his livelihood but he was twice the elected Assessor for Swan River Township. The first term was 1937-1938; the second term was 1939-1940. His brother Russell Blair credits him with keeping the best records they ever had. He was often called upon for advice from friends and family.

Our parents attended the local schools in their areas and each completed the eighth grade. Going to high school in Little Falls was out of the question for them because he had to work on the farm and Mom's parents didn't have the one dollar a month for her transportation. Most country kids had to live with relatives in town to attend high school. It must be remembered that these were the years of the Great Depression.

They both attended a dance in Little Falls. She was fourteen years old and this was one of the first dances she attended. Our dad says he saw her walking across the room and thought she was the finest woman he had ever laid eyes on. At the time he didn't know how young she was. He thought she was much older plus she fibbed a little on her end. She was not the giddy, silly girl that most fourteen-year-old girls are.

The Blair farm was located about eight miles southwest of Little Falls and Mom was living about fifteen miles north of Little Falls. Twenty-three miles on rutted dirt roads was quite a distance to travel to do much courting which could only happen after his chores were done. They were married on a very cold day, January 6, 1936 in St. Stanislaus Catholic Church, in Sobieski, Minnesota which was the church that our dad and the family attended.

Wedding Picture

Left: Alois Pierzina, Helen Hankes,
Witnesses: Ruby Hankes and Clarence Pierzina

Newspaper article that appeared in Little Falls paper reads as follows:

Happenings around Swan River section

"A large number from here motored to Sobieski and attended the shower for Miss Helen Hankes and Alois Pierzina which was held Thursday evening. They received many beautiful gifts. The wedding took place Monday."

The wedding dinner was held at the Peter Blair farm. Alois's grandparents, Peter Blair was French, born in Quebec, Canada where they spoke only French. Grandmother Emma Wieczorek Blair was born in Germany making an interesting combination of cultures. Our mother remembers that sauerkraut was served. In those days, the three meals a day were called breakfast, dinner, and supper; and Emma always included the sauerkraut with every meal, but hopefully not for breakfast.

After their marriage, they lived with grandparents Peter and Emma until March, 1936. They moved onto a farm which was a short distance from the Blair farm and was on the same road as Alois's other grandparents, John and Johanna (Czech) Pierzina, who lived just a short distance away. This farm was relatively small and the rent was $100 per year. The house was not large and there was no running water, but there was the usual indoor pump bringing forth water from the well. There was no electricity, telephone, or indoor plumbing so there was no bathroom. Only the first three children, Dwaine, Bette and Dianne lived on this farm.

Daddy's father, George Pierzina, moved in with them on the same day they moved onto the Swan River farm, and Louise continued to live with her parents. On October 24, 1938, George's father, John Pierzina died. In those days, the coffins were kept in the family homes and not at a funeral parlor. It has been described to us that George was cleaning and sweeping around his dad's coffin on the morning of his dad's burial, when suddenly he wheeled around the broom, fell to the floor, and never walked again. George suffered a stroke and was paralyzed for the rest of his life. He was taken to the hospital and the burial of his father went on as scheduled. Although paralyzed and bedridden, George continued to live with our parents until we moved to Randall in 1941. He went to live with our dad's cousin Pauline Wozniak until he died on April 10, 1943. He used a bell to summon help when he needed something. Because he was my Godfather, I was given this bell after he died but unfortunately, I no longer have it.

8

There were six children born to Alois and Helen. We were born between the years 1936 and 1945 and all were born in St. Gabriel's Hospital in Little Falls, Minnesota. The first born was Dwaine and I was their second child and first daughter. There were two sisters and two brothers that followed: Dianne, Judith, Russell, and George. Our dad chose Dwaine's name. He went to work in the corn fields in Iowa where he worked with someone with that name and liked it. My mother went into the hospital intending to name me Darla if I were a girl, but I came home with the name Elizabeth Ann, named after the attending nun, but I'm commonly known as Bette. I was born at 7:00 a.m. and weighed 8 pounds. Dwaine my older brother was born at 8:00 a.m. and weighed 7 pounds, so our birth weights and time were easy to remember. My parents intended for my middle name to be Anne, but the doctor left off the 'e' and he misspelled Dianne's name with Dionne but she had it corrected years later. I just took on the name Ann, although I would have preferred it the intended way. Thanks Dr. Fortier, for that chicken scratch handwriting that only a doctor can read.

Our dad had what is called a 'Simian Line' in both his hands. A Simian line is when the line goes straight across the palm of the hand without a break in it. It is believed to be of Bohemian origin and gypsies of old refused to read these palms. Of his six children, five have this same line. Some have it in both palms and some in one palm only. Mom did not have this trait and most people don't.

St. Gabriel's Hospital

Catholic hospital operated by the Franciscan Nuns.

Two hospital bills, Dwaine's and Dianne's, show a portion of Dwaine's bill was paid for with potatoes. His total hospital bill was $30.00. Dianne's bill reads as follows:

6 days in sickroom @ $2.50/day	$15.00
Supplies	$5.00
Medicine and lotion	$1.50
Surgical dressings	$3.00
Care of baby	$3.00
Total	$27.50
Credit for hog 280 lbs. @ 7 ½ cents per pound	$21.00
Balance due: paid in cash on June 20, 1940	$6.50
Doctor bill of $25 was paid in full July 5, 1940	$25.00

Mom was a very young bride when they married. She was fifteen years old when Dwaine was born and our father was twenty-four. Mom didn't have the luxury of getting on the telephone and calling her mother, whether to chat or learn how to make something. She had to experiment or relied on our father for advice. He even taught her how to bake bread. For the most part, she had to learn it on her own, whether it was making gravy, or how to care for a sick child—and a sick child she certainly did have!!

When Dianne was three-to-four months old, she became very ill with what was called a "stomach complaint." She was taken off all milk and milk products and was fed strained oatmeal. Dr. Fortier was ready to send her to the University Hospital but wanted to try one last remedy. It was a form of gruel and the effects worked immediately. Dianne had become extremely emaciated and skeletal but she recovered and thrived after that and gained weight very fast. Looking back, Mom realized how dangerously sick she was and wonders how she ever survived.

Dianne was almost a year old when Doctor Fortier feared that she had diphtheria. She had diphtheria-like symptoms and Mom remembers how her chest literally caved into her backbone when she took a breath. She was hospitalized from the 25th to the 28th of March 1941. Her hospital bill reads as follows: Notice how expensive the oxygen was even then.

3 days board in sickroom @ $3.50/day	$10.50
Medicine and lotion	$.75
Oxygen for 24 hours @ .75/hour	$18.00
Antitoxin – no charge	$0
Total	$29.25

Receipt dated May 3, 1941, shows that this bill was paid in full by "potatoes to convent."

When the diapers got soiled with urine only, mom would rinse them out and then hang them over the stove to dry, enabling her to keep a relatively clean one handy because she didn't have a large supply of them. This was a practice that was done by almost all of the mothers. She remembers one woman who was making gravy and the diaper fell in the pan of gravy, so the woman picked it up, wrung the diaper out, and served the gravy.

Mom

Caught off guard at back door wearing her apron.

In the early years, she didn't have a washing machine, so Mom had to wash clothes on a scrub board. Before the washing could begin, she had to pump the water into a large container, heat it on the stove, and then transfer the water into tubs, one for washing and one for rinsing.

She still remembers how hard it was washing the overalls on that scrub board trying to get them clean, which she says was almost impossible to do. Not only did she have to do laundry for a husband, toddlers and baby, but she also cared for her now invalid father-in-law George, who was still living with them. Our dad took care of George's personal hygiene and bathing, but she was in charge of the bedding and clothing and she was all of eighteen years old. Grandpa George loved it when Dwaine would sit on the bed with him and keep him company. When Dwaine would tire of sitting there and try to get down, his grandpa would ask him to stay longer. Dwaine remembers our dad carrying his father with a blanket wrapped around him because there were people visiting, giving George the opportunity to be in their company.

She also got the experience of cooking for a work crew. A neighboring farmer named Sepurek owned a threshing machine. They went from farm-to-farm at harvest time with a crew of about six men to cut and thresh the crops that were in the fields. When the crew finished working on Daddy's cousin Pauline Wozniak's farm down the road a bit, Mom and Daddy knew that they would be arriving at our farm next. That's when the cooking in the kitchen started and getting everything ready to feed them all, which included friends and neighbors who lent a hand.

On Mom's first attempt at cooking for them, she remembers as being pretty disastrous. On this day the crew arrived in the early evening so they spent the night in the barn. Mom was only fifteen years old and still very inexperienced. She got up before daylight and started cooking them breakfast. This was fairly easy because she had eggs from the chickens and pancakes. For lunch she remembers that she cooked rings of bologna, potatoes and for dessert, she served them prunes. Her cooking abilities improved with the years and they always looked forward to coming to our farm because they knew they were going to get a good meal and be well-fed.

Along with cows and chickens, there were pigs on the farm. The male is called a boar and the female is called a sow. One day our dad was with one of his sows while she was giving birth to her piglets. Two of them appeared to be born dead. He wrapped them in a gunny sack, brought them into the house and put them in a tub of warm water; there was always a pan of warm water on the stove. While in the warm water, he massaged their hearts. Both babies were revived but they were rejected by their mother. Mom and Daddy then wrapped the baby pigs in a blanket and put them in their bed with them for warmth. Only one survived and grew into a very large pig.

Team of horses in full harness

The horses on the farm were unpredictable and always running away. They were wild western horses, freshly broken in the Dakotas, and they didn't make good work horses. One day our dad had just unhooked the team from the mower when they broke and ran with their harnesses still on them, still hooked together with leather strapping. Dwaine was just a toddler when he was playing outside on the porch. Mom aware of the commotion going on outside ran to the door and grabbed Dwaine and brought him inside the house. At that moment, the still-harnessed horses were running so fast they couldn't stop; they ran right up onto the porch where Dwaine had just been standing. When they tried to stop, they skidded across the porch and didn't come to a halt until they hit the wall of the house. They lay there for some time with their sides heaving.

We were always cautioned that when there was lightning about, we were never to stand under a tree. There was a time when our dad did that. He was out with a team of horses that were hooked to a stone-boat. A stone-boat is a large flat board used to easily roll large rocks on without lifting them; it looks like a low-profile sled. A sudden storm came up, so he drove the horses to the shelter of a very large oak tree for them to stay under until the storm passed. While he was waiting, he laid down on the empty stone-boat to take a little nap. That's when his nightmare began. Lightening first stuck the tree they were under and exited it by ripping up the ground, making a furrow for quite a distance. The horses bolted and ran with our dad still on the stone-boat, hanging on to nothing for the wild ride of his life and being at the mercy of the frightened horses. The horses headed straight for home. They ran into the barn and in their stalls with the stone-boat and our dad still hooked to their harnesses.

The stone boat was also used as a means of transportation when the family visited with others that lived nearby. When the front of the stone-boat was attached to the harness, it lifted the front end up, preventing it from digging into the ground. There were no seats to sit on, so hay and blankets were spread out and the driver could only stand while directing the team of horses. What a bumpy, dusty ride that must have been being so near the ground. In the summer months we had to cross a very small stream which usually meant that those on the stone-boat got a spraying of water. It gave a much smoother ride in the winter snow.

Dwaine had a walker that he was put into as a toddler until he learned to walk. The top which hit him at his waistline was not much larger than his waist and he was able to hold onto the wooden rim. The bottom of this walker had a very wide circumference with wheels that just cleared the doorways with about a half inch to spare on each side. He wouldn't try to walk on his own, but when trying to get through a doorway, he would lift the whole walker up to step over the door sill. He couldn't walk but he could carry the walker.

Dwaine began walking on his first birthday. I took my first steps on his birthday also, which was July 1st. My parents remembering back to the day that we both started walking said, "Wouldn't it be funny if Dianne started walking today, too." Dianne looked at them with a grin and took off walking. All three of the oldest children took their first steps on July 1st.

When Dwaine was first learning to talk, he didn't or couldn't say, "Daddy, Father or Dad," he called our father "Di." Throughout all our lives all six of us also called him Di. So Dwaine is responsible for the unique nickname. Mom mostly called us by our proper names but sometimes she would call me Liz, but Daddy had a nickname for each of us. Little red-headed Dwaine was called Skipper. Uncle Russell Pierzina, who later became Russell Blair, first called him that because when he walked, he had a skip to his step. I was called Bess, Dianne was called Weasel, Judy was called Judariska, Russell and George were both called Skunk but we used to tease George unmercifully with Georgie Porgie.

16

Little Boy Blue

Mom entered a contest with this picture of Dwaine and called it "LITTLE BOY BLUE" and won $5.00 for it, which at that time was a good sum of money. Following is the nursery rhyme. Although in this case he was on top the haystack.

Little Boy Blue come blow your horn,
The sheep's in the meadow the cow's in the corn.
But where is the boy who looks after the sheep?
He's under a haystack fast asleep.
Will you wake him?
No, not I
For if I do, he's sure to cry.

Our baby bottles were like a soda pop bottle and in all probability was a pop bottle with a narrow neck and a ridge at the top. The nipple, which was called a rubber teat, was pulled tightly over the ridge. There weren't any rings or means to tighten it down so with a good pull the youngster could pull the nipple off and most likely meant an end to their bottle days because of the cleanup that would come from that. Dwaine learned a valuable lesson of 'thou shall not steal' little sister's baby bottle. He still carries a large scar on his foot when he took the bottle that belonged to either Bette or Dianne and he dropped it breaking it into a lot of little pieces. Being a barefoot little boy, he stepped on the broken glass and cut himself pretty severely.

Sometimes chickens can be mean and sneaky, especially a different breed than the regular white chickens. They wander the yard acting nonchalant and when nobody is looking they jump on you and dig their claws in. Then, they go back to eating as though nothing has happened. There was a very large black chicken, which Dwaine remembers it being as tall as he was. Not likely to have been a rooster because roosters had no value on a farm except to fatten them up and becoming a delicious meal. He remembers that he was always the target of this chicken when nobody was looking. It always seemed to lay in wait for him and when he was halfway between the house and the barn it would ambush him, digging his claws into him. One day when he got jumped, it knocked him to the ground and attacked his face, cutting him up badly. Mom was afraid he was going to be scarred for life, but he did heal in time, and was not scarred. Our dad immediately butchered the chicken and Dwaine was so glad and so relieved to see the end of that chicken. He says that it became a delicious meal and was the best chicken he ever ate in his whole life.

Mom at fourteen years old when she was courting

Rats will sometimes move in packs and a pack of rats migrated onto this farm. Trying to get rid of the rodents was quite a battle. One night when Dianne was still a baby she was sleeping for the night. The rats got up into the crib with her, under the covers, and chewed on her legs. She carried the scars all her life, although not noticeable in later years. Mom woke up one night with one dancing on her chest which scared the daylights out of her, as one can only imagine. In a very short time we moved from this farm. We lived on this farm from March to March, for exactly five years.

**Mom at
Grandfather John Pierzina's**

Dwaine

Now where is that dog farm?

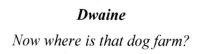

**Mom's sister Della
Hankes, Dwaine, and
Mom**

Dwaine with kitty

Dad and Dwaine

Dad must have a special treat in hand for Dwaine.

Dwaine and Daddy

Riding brother Russell's new bicycle.

Dwaine

Now where is that dog?

Grandma Louise Pierzina, Mom, and Great grandma

Emma Blair holding Bette
Picture taken at Peter Blair farm, not far from the farm we lived on.

Bet Dwaine's thinking, 'She looks like a cry baby to me.'

Bette sitting up

**Dwaine, Joanne Pierzina, Bette at Grandma and Grandpa
Hankes**

***Grandma Hankes holding Joanne Pierzina—Dwaine and
Bette on each side (Uncle Orlo Hankes in back)***

Dwaine with the pigs

***Joanne Pierzina, Marie Becker, Louise (Weezie) Becker
holding Dianne, Bette, Dwaine***

Picture taken at Grandma and Grandpa Hankes.

1940

***Grandma Louise with seven of her children and their
spouses (Son, George is missing)***

*Flossie with Frank, Howard with Rachael, Louise Pierzina,
Alois with Helen, Clarence with Ruby.
Doodie, Russell and Ione Becker all single.*

26

Our Mom,
Helen Pierzina

❧ Chapter Two ❧

Our Farm

The date was March 16, 1941, when we all moved to the farm in Darling Township at Rural Route #1, Randall, Minnesota. The purchase price was $10,000. Mr. Johnson, the previous owner paid $10,000 just for the building of the barn. The farm was in foreclosure when our parents bought it. This was to become our childhood home. Two-hundred-sixty-five acres were lying at our feet for us to romp and play on. There were no visible farms or homes that could be seen in any direction. We were totally and completely private.

This picture appears to have been taken when the farm was first bought. It seems that the previous owner left an awful mess behind. Dwaine remembers that there was a lot of concrete that had to be removed. This had to be a hard, very busy summer, trying to settle in, get the crops in the ground, plant a garden, build a chicken house, prepare for new baby, and clean up this mess. Makes you wonder how they did it. It would be interesting to know what the inside of the house looked like.

Our farm was situated between Little Falls and Randall. About fifteen miles from Little Falls and about seven miles from Randall. County Road 210, the road to our farm was a dirt road, not even graveled, just dirt. You could see a car coming because the dust cloud was visible for a long way off. We knew they were coming to our house because rarely did a car just pass by. It also gave us a chance to get things in order before our parents returned home. That could be anything from tidying up to trying to fix whatever we broke to getting the animals fed, which we were supposed to have done earlier.

From Little Falls, as you neared our farm, you had to cross over a bridge to get across the Little Elk River. After crossing the bridge the river was on your right. It was a small river but large enough to always have moving water in it; it never ran dry and it eventually deposited into the Mississippi River. On the left was our sheep pasture.

We only raised sheep for the first few years, but the sheep pasture retained its name. Raising sheep was more work than it was worth. They were always jumping fences and were a nuisance. I recall our dad spending many nights with the sheep because they required a lot of care during the birth of the lambs. Often the lambs were born in the winter with the weather too severe for them to survive without help. Many times, he brought the new lambs into the house because they were often rejected by their mothers. These babies were called "bummers" and they required a lot of care. They were kept in boxes by the stove for warmth and had to be hand fed. The sheep pasture was marshy and lightly wooded. This area was so pretty with lots of frogs, Whooping Cranes, and full of every kind of song bird that Minnesota has to offer.

View of our farm from the bend in the road

Picture taken before improvements of silo and chicken house.

Continuing down County Road 210 and around the bend, you could see our farm off to the left. Our fields were on both sides of this road which actually ran through the middle of our land. If you continued straight past our driveway the road would lead to Randall and our mailbox. Upon reaching our driveway, you're at a four-corner crossroad. To the right was the road that led to the cow pasture and to the left was the long driveway to our home. We had to cross this county road to take the cows to the pasture.

Farm after improvements of silo and chicken house

When driving down the driveway and entering the yard to the left was the chicken house. Looking straight ahead was a large red barn in a very pretty setting with a large grove of pine trees toward the back half of the barn and encompassed one side of the cow pen where the cows stayed after being let out after milking. To the right was a large two story white house. On the other side of the house was another grove of pine trees that were good for climbing and made excellent shelter from the rain while we played house and many other games. Our dad hung an old bed spring between the trees and that gave us hours of play. There were also large Box Elder trees in the front yard. Behind the house was a long row of fragrant lilac bushes. The orchard was also behind the house, with a variety of plum and apple trees. Also bushes that produced currants and berries that Mom turned into wonderful jams and jellies.

Our House
Upstairs window was the girl's bedroom.

The front of the house had a large bay window that gave it a very nice style. Across half the house was an enclosed porch where we hung our coats and cracked hazel nuts, better known as filberts that we picked from bushes in the cow pasture. We'd bring home gunny sacks full of the nuts and spread them out to dry until their moist outside hulls dried up and the nut would easily break away.

Although our house was very large, basically three big rooms comprised the bottom floor. The kitchen was very, very large. The other two rooms, a living room and our parents' bedroom, were almost as large. There was also a pantry and one very small room used for a winter bedroom. There was no electricity, running water, telephone, or indoor plumbing. In the kitchen there was a pump on a sturdy table that provided us our water. During the night all the water would drain out back into the well; so we always made sure that there was a pitcher full of water to "prime the pump" in the morning. Water from the pitcher was poured back into the pump to replace the air that filled the pipes during the night. Pumping very fast, water came back out of the spout; otherwise you could pump all day and only get air.

The second story where we had our bedrooms was never finished. The walls were up and had slats on them for lath and plaster, but the plaster was never applied. The upstairs had a musty, woodsy smell that was not at all unpleasant. In the daytime it was a very relaxing place to pass the time; but at night time, it could be very spooky. Dianne, Judy, and I shared one room while the boys shared the other. The remainder of the upstairs was used for storage, although there weren't a lot of things stored, it was almost empty. In the winter we would wake up in the morning and there could be snow on the floor where the howling wind blew it in. Although well built, some small cracks must not have been sealed. The windows were single pane glass and there didn't seem to be any insulation around them.

Dianne and Judy in the kitchen

Notice the pump for water next to the door leading to the pantry and the wood-burning cook stove.

During the coldest months in winter we all slept downstairs. We shared two bunk beds in the little room. On one wall was the boy's bunk where Russell and George shared the top bunk and Dwaine got the bottom one to himself. On the other wall were the girls' bunks, Dianne and I shared the top bunk and Judy got the bottom one to herself. I remember one night, I was moaning and groaning and found myself lying on the floor; Mom came in and helped me. I don't remember if I went back up to the top bunk or just crawled in with Judy.

Our heating stove was small and wasn't big enough to hold enough wood to stay burning all night. In the morning, our parents poured the kerosene into it and got it roaring so hot the sides of the stove glowed a bright red. We all gathered around it to dress in the mornings. As we faced the stove, the heat was intensely hot, while the back side of our body was chilled with the cold air still in the room.

We also had a spooky basement. The walls were concrete but the floor was dirt. We were always sure there was a monster of some sort down there. There was no electricity, so our only source of light was a lantern that we hung on a nail in the stairwell. The light was suspended from a nail and would move to and fro and because it was a kerosene lantern, it would flicker. With each flicker we were sure that behind each piece of wood in the woodpile something was going to jump out.

The stairs had open steps and even if the monster didn't get us at the woodpile, he surely would grab us through the open step we were on, or the next one. We couldn't lift our feet fast enough to make it to safety into the kitchen. We were in such a hurry to get out of there, rather than get an armful of wood, we'd grab one piece and run. Therefore, we had to make trip after dreaded trip down the steps before we finally had enough wood to build a fire the next morning. It was the same when we had to put coal in a bucket to take upstairs.

This was a large basement, as large as the house. There were two main compartments in the basement. Going down the stairs was where the coal and wood pile were located with one pile on each side of the steps. We used either one to heat the house but only wood was used in the cook stove.

34

From this area there was a doorway that led to another room where food was stored. It was located by going around to the back of the steps. This also was a large room with a dirt floor that was divided. One side was for our canned goods, with shelves for all the glass jars which contained the fruits and vegetables that had grown during the summer months and then canned. Potatoes, bushel baskets of apples, rutabagas, etc. were stored all winter in the other half of this room and stayed fresh for several months. Both areas were kept dark and cool. A lantern was always carried for our light source. We didn't have a refrigerator so this room was where we kept our food that required being cool. To keep food cold, we used the icy water in the milk room that was part of the barn. Grandma Pierzina had an ice box that held a large block of ice that was delivered to her house every few days, but we didn't have an ice box. Maybe that was a good thing because it would be a lot of work to keep the water contained and cleaned up that the

melted ice would generate. It would be much easier to carry our food to the milk room.

Mom caught coming out of the outhouse

The outhouse—biffy or toilet as they were called—was a small building that stood a short distance from the house, measuring about 4 feet by 6 feet. Every year we got a new Montgomery Ward and Sears & Roebuck catalog so the old ones were taken to the outhouse and that became our toilet paper, always avoiding the stiff, colored pages. A real treat was when we bought a crate of peaches which were packaged in a nice soft tissue. If toilet tissue had been invented yet, it hadn't found its way to our farm or anybody else we knew. The saying was that you knew who was wealthy by the size outhouse they had, whether they had two holes or one. Some had a smaller hole for children, but we had to learn to fend for ourselves.

Cousin Jim Hankes remembers when he was in the outhouse and Russell climbed on the roof and was jumping around while George was doing something outside just as irritating. He says they didn't know he was going to be bigger than them one day.

In the center of the yard was a portable type of building where the new chicks were kept in the spring time. This was called a brooder. They required very warm quarters and this was easy to heat. It was so much fun to go in there where it was toasty warm, and hundreds of little yellow balls of fur would climb all over you. Every one of us had fallen asleep in there because it was so warm and comfortable. The chicks develop feathers in a short amount of time and then are allowed out of the brooder. We always had to be on the lookout for chicken hawks because they would swoop down and grab the chicks. Mom or Daddy would come running with a gun. Mom never missed a target or rodent even into and surpassing her eighty years of life. Initially there were several hundred chicks purchased but from the flock, there were going to be losses. Some would not survive because of elements and predators and some were roosters, which we butchered because only egg laying hens were kept.

Daddy on trailer shoveling sawdust in chicken house, Dianne and Judy on ground

This insulated the building and no heat source was utilized.

Our dad built the chicken house, a building large enough to house a few hundred chickens. Inside was a feed room that held the oats, ground-up corn, and oyster shells that improved the quality and hardness of the egg shells. We also stored the eggs in this room after they were gathered.

In the main part of this building, the center was fairly empty except for the feeders that were set in long rows up off the floor. A well had been dug and there was a pump with a handle that we pumped the water for them. There were two walls which held dozens of wooden boxes. These were the nests where the chickens would go to lay their eggs. Sometimes they dropped them wherever they happened to be, but the floor was covered with straw. Each chicken generally laid one egg a day. The young chickens were called pullets and when they began laying eggs, they were very small, somewhat bigger than a bird egg, but as the chicken grew larger in size so did the egg.

On one side of the building was their roosting area. It was very long and deep and was sloped. It was higher in back and lowered in front with slats going across the width. This gave the chickens a foothold and they could sit steady while they slept. They slept with their heads tucked under their wings. The flooring of this rack had chicken wire stretched across where the manure fell through to the cement floor but the chickens couldn't fall or go into the waste. This was cleaned every so often and the chicken manure was stored in a pile at the edge of the field and used as fertilizer for the crops. Every spring before the new chicks were allowed in, the rack was dismantled and the entire chicken house was cleaned and thoroughly fumigated

After the young chicks developed feathers, they were turned loose and could go to the chicken house. Not only were they fed their chicken feed from the Co-Op, they were also allowed to grow and grub for food in the yard. They were free to roam all summer. In the evening they'd roost in the branches of the trees, under the shed or anywhere they chose. As the hot, humid summer faded into cool weather, we had to gather all the chickens and put them in the chicken house.

They had to be confined in the winter—otherwise they'd freeze to death. We would go out after dark and every one of us was out catching chickens. They'd be sleeping, so we would reach under and grab them by the leg and they'd squawk and scratch and try to get away. It always took half the night before we finally finished and before our bloody hands and arms got tended to. What we missed we soon found the next day because they were the only ones in the yard but eventually they were caught too.

The eggs had to be taken from a sometimes nasty chicken that pecked at our hands when we tried to reach under them to gather them. Before the eggs could be sold they were put in a tub of warm soapy water and washed. We washed hundreds—if not thousands—of eggs. Then they were put in flats and taken to town and sold to a Co-Op in Randall. Usually Mom was the one who took them.

Chickens are really pretty dumb creatures. When the sun goes down and it's getting dusk, they head for the roosting rack to spend the night but that could be as early as four or five o'clock in the afternoon in the winter. They stay there until the first ray of daylight the next morning. It would have been a benefit to keep them up longer to improve egg production.

After we got electricity the chicken house was wired with lights that went the length of the building. As long as the lights were on they would not roost and would stay up all night. We needed to find a way to keep them up longer but not all night.

Our dad set up a timer that turned the lights on in the late afternoon and a second timer that came on about 8:00 pm. This second timer turned on a very large light bulb that when it was on, it used the bulk of the electricity, causing the other lights in the building to go dim. When the lights dimmed and remained dim for about fifteen minutes, it gave the chickens ample time to make their way to roost and then the timer would turn off all the lights including the large bulb and the building became dark.

This would have worked well except that the bright light gave off too much light in the room and they wouldn't go to the roosting rack. Then when the timer shut off all the lights including the bright one, it left them in total darkness and they were not smart enough or had good enough vision to find the rack.

So to keep the bright light from being so bright, our dad put a gunny sack over it. A gunny sack is an inexpensive bag made of burlap used for transporting grains, potatoes, and other products. For a smart man, he did a pretty dumb thing. That was almost a disastrous choice on his part because one morning when they went into the chicken house, they found that the gunny sack was charred and burned. The whole building of chickens could have gone up in a fire and we would have been eating burned chicken and charred feathers for months to come. He rewired the bright light and moved it into the feed room and then he shut the door. Everything worked smoothly after that.

Although we raised ordinary white chickens, there was one year that we got some Rhode Island Reds. They were a very large, dark red bird. I was about five years old when I went to the chicken house with my dad to help him feed the chickens. He was always so full of praise when we did a good job so it was a pleasure to work with him. There were several red roosters in that flock. They were tall enough to look me right in the eyes, and they weren't afraid of anything. I was pumping water for them when my dad turned his back to go into the feed room and a sneaky rooster jumped on me raking me with his claws. He got me from my face down to my waist. I was bleeding, scared, my dress was torn and did I let out a scream! My dad grabbed the rooster and snapped its neck. Then he got rid of the rest by butchering all of them.

Our barn was large and it was a nice one. As you entered through the front double doors, on the left was the tool room. This is where hammers and wrenches, shovels, etc. were kept. Next to the tool room was a walkway that led to the manger. After the hay was thrown down from the loft, it was put in the manger for the cows. This walkway was also used to access the silo after it was built.

There was a long row of stanchions the remaining length of the barn. The stanchions held each cow in her own place for milking and they lived in the barn all winter. In the spring when the cows were let out into the cow pen they were frisky as calves. They'd been confined to the barn and even the oldest heifers showed their pleasure when released by jumping, kicking, and running around.

On the opposite side of the barn, entering through the double doors, on the right was a stairway that led to the hayloft and a pen located next to and under the steps was where we kept a bull.

Next to that bullpen was a stall large enough for our two horses, Dick and Queenie. Queenie was a gentle mare while Dick could be not so gentle. Next to the horse stall was a pen where the pigs were kept but only when they were expecting young, otherwise they stayed in the pig pen behind the barn and on the other side of the cow pen.

There was a walkway that led to a doorway into the milk room where the milk was stored. This room was built by our dad and was not an original part of the barn. He also set up a shower system in there so that was where we could take a shower. The remainder of that side of the barn contained several more stanchions.

There wasn't any kind of heating system in the barn. It was kept warm by the body heat and breathing of the animals and was never cold. The hayloft got cold in the winter, but all the hay served as insulation for the lower part of the barn. Two or three lanterns were hung on posts to provide light.

The floor of the barn was cemented and was wide enough to easily drive a wagon through to the double doors on each end. A wagon was used when it was time to clean out the gutter. Using a scoop shovel, the manure was scooped out of the gutter and thrown onto the wagon. The gutter was at the back end of the cows and ran the whole length of the stanchions area. You quickly became watchful where you stepped. One misstep in the gutter and you had manure as high as your ankle. We didn't accidently step in them very often. Each cow was bedded down with fresh straw every night and the old straw went on the wagon with the manure. The manure was then made into a pile at the edge of the field and later put in a spreader which evenly distributed it and was used as fertilizer for the new crops in the spring.

Each cow knew which stanchion was hers. The younger ones would go to any one they chose, but the older seasoned cows didn't like it when a young cow got into their space, and would wedge the younger one out. The younger one would move from stanchion to stanchion until she found one that was not already taken and could stay there. They got their drinking water from a fountain that was located between two cows and the two shared the same fountain. They pressed their mouths down on a lever plate and water that was piped in came to the surface and they drank their fill. A water tank was located in the hayloft and water flowed by gravity.

A cow had to give birth to a calf every year to keep up milk production otherwise she would give a lesser amount of milk. Before a young heifer could produce any milk, she first had to be bred and give birth. If the heifer proved to be infertile, she was sold along with the young bulls.

We had about eighteen cows that had to be milked morning and evening. When it came time to milk a cow, we had to wash her first, mainly the bag and teats. Then the milkman or woman sat on a one-legged stool which had only a single post going down the center with a flat board on top. When Dwaine first began the job of milking, the stool was a little too high for him and he remembers a couple of times losing his balance. One time he went over backwards and found himself looking up at the underbelly of the cow next to him. Once the leg was cut shorter, he was always able to maintain his balance.

When the milking was being done, the pail was normally held between the knees; but in Dwaine's earlier days, he had to set the pail on the floor. A well-placed kick by the cow would send the pail full of milk and Dwaine flying. He had to move quickly to catch the pail and the stool and stay on his feet. When a cow proved to be a kicker, she had to be hobbled with 'kickers' on her back legs. One time a very feisty cow kicked so hard she pulled her other leg out from under herself and fell to the floor. This caused her to panic and it became quite a job getting her upright again. The older cows never kicked, it was only the young ones.

After we got electricity, we got an electric milking machine which cut down the milking time considerably. Two cows could be milked at the same time now. There were two units, each with four suction cups which were placed on the teats, and the milk came through long hoses attached to a receiving canister that sat in the middle of the barn floor. It was necessary to keep close watch because when the cow had given up all her milk, the suction cups would no longer stay in place and could fall to the floor. Then they had to be carefully washed.

We always liked to have Dwaine or our dad squirt milk in our mouths while we stood about six feet away. The milk tasted different from each cow. The cats liked it too. After we got the electric milking machine, we could no longer do that.

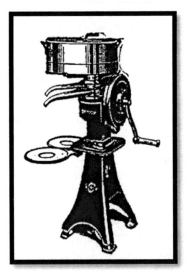

Cream Separator

After the cows were milked, the milk was taken to the milk room and put through a separator. The milk was poured into a container on top and by turning the crank it separated the milk from the cream. It's an amazing operation when you think about it. Milk came out of one spout and cream out of the other, each going into a separate can. There were many little disks and filters that the milk went through and they had to be washed thoroughly after the separating was done. The cream was stored in a smaller can and the milk went into large milk cans and they were stored in a cooler.

The cooler was a large, round, wooden container that our dad built. It was filled with ice cold water from an underground well. The milk stayed in the icy water until the milk truck came for it about every other day. It was then taken to Little Falls and sold to the creamery. When they made a return trip, they brought us our butter and dairy products that we had ordered; sometimes it might even be ice cream but not too often, we had no way to keep it frozen. Butter cost a nickel a pound from the creamery and was stored in a sealed bucket and kept in the same icy water as the milk. Randall got a meat processing facility that rented out freezer space to the public which we used and were very glad to have, but if you needed a pound of hamburger the drive to get it was seven miles away.

1932 Chevy car taking a wagon load of corn to the pigs in their pigpen

The barn also housed the pigs when they had a new litter, otherwise they lived in the pig pen. Each mother pig gave birth to about eight-to-ten piglets. Shortly before the litter was born, a mother pig was separated from the rest of the pigs and put in a pen by herself. This was done for her safety as well as the newborns because they had to be protected from the male pigs—or bores, as they were called.

The sow was very protective of her young and never wanted us to touch them. When the baby got close to the edge of the pen, we'd grab one or two and run up to the hayloft with them. To get to the hayloft from where the pen was, we had to climb a ladder but the lowest rung was more than three feet off the floor, so we had to climb on the horse manger and reach for the ladder that was attached to the wall. Above this ladder was an opening in the floor of the hayloft which we crawled through with the squirming baby pig in our arms. After getting them into the loft, we'd put baby or doll clothes on the piglets and try to hug them, but they didn't like it. They weren't very good at all for cuddling. They just squealed and squirmed while their mama got noisier and madder downstairs. We'd eventually slip them back into the pen, but we never dared take our eyes off her. We had good reason to be wary of her. Our dad did not know, and would have given us a spanking, but of course he was out of sight when we did that.

One day our bull was in the mix of the cows and went with them to the cow pasture when they were turned out to graze. Usually this bull was kept closer to home because he was a good bull, producing fine calves and he was an expensive one. The bull didn't return home with the cows at the end of the day. Our parents looked for the bull but couldn't find it. Our dad offered a reward of $25 for his safe return, which was announced on the radio. Many of the locals were out looking for it hoping to cash in on the reward.

Bull that was lost in the pasture, now kept closer to home in the cow pen

He was dehorned so he couldn't gore us.

Finally our dad rented an airplane and the pilot flew over the area. They made one pass over the cow pasture and found him. A part of the cow pasture was so thick of brush and marsh and swampland that it was almost impossible to get through it. What had happened was the bull was in the water and he stepped on his chain and couldn't move or get out. One of the neighbors, Tony Wenzel thought that maybe he could find it, and when our dad returned home after the airplane trip, he encountered Tony leading the bull home, who it seems he just grabbed a hold of the chain and the bull followed him out. He tried to pay Tony the reward but Tony would not take any money from Loysey as he called him.

Dwaine remembers the first year we were on this farm and our dad bought a young bull that he was going to butcher later in the year; so, to fatten it up, our dad castrated him. Dwaine was in the barn area with the new steer and he realized that something was dreadfully wrong with the animal. Our dad was in the field with the team of horses cutting the hay. We were never allowed in the field when this chore was being done because of the danger of getting cut from the sharp blades that were hidden close to the ground, but he went to the field anyway to get our dad even though he was afraid he would get in trouble. They immediately returned back to the barn yard and found that the steer was bleeding excessively and had to be put down. The meat had to be butchered and processed right away. The only option was to can the meat because we didn't have a freezer and the facility had not yet opened in Randall. So in the hot, humid summer weather the wood burning cook stove had to be fired up and the work began. Dwaine remembers that Mom was at the stove and passed out onto the floor and Daddy was very excited in trying to revive her. She would have been in her seventh month of pregnancy with Judy. He remembers that the job got finished because he saw rows and rows of canned meat on the shelves in the basement.

For the most part the whole farm was pretty flat land. Our yard was also flat except for a rise where the house stood and a hill that crested to another field. Nestled in the hill was a building with three walls and a roof, where the machinery was stored. It kept the weather away from the equipment and was usually cool in the summer because the breezes flowed through it. Our dad had a grinding stone that was a revolving stone disk, used for sharpening his tools and blades. He usually did those kinds of chores in this building. Shortly before we moved from the farm we had a heavy snowfall and the roof collapsed, so it was eventually torn down. In back of the building and a little ways away were the corn crib and the gravel pit. Blue bells grew in abundance up on that hill.

In the winter this hill became higher at the top because the wind would blow across the field causing the snow to form a bank making it steeper in the winter than in summer, so it was a good place to ride our sleds. Our sleds had runners on them, but if the snow was soft it would just dig down into the snow. If there was a hardened surface on the snow we got a pretty good ride all the way down into the yard. We also used a scoop shovel to sit on and that worked better in soft snow because it offered a wide flat surface on the snow. In the summer we would crawl in an old tire and get rolled down the hill which worked pretty good if someone else helped guide it.

The last building was the grain shed that sat up a little hill near the barn. This was where the grinding machine was kept. The wheat or corn was fed into the machine, which was then pounded and ground into smaller grain to be fed to the chickens and animals. We usually weren't allowed in that building when they were working because of the small quarters and so many moving parts, and because it was hard to breathe with the dust and hulls flying around the room. A hole was cut in the wall to hook the belt to the tractors belt pulley, which is a spinning wheel to make it run. The tractor was parked a short distance away with the brakes locked. You learned to generate power when it was needed when you didn't have electricity.

One evening Dwaine remembers seeing a ball of lightning traveling on the ground as it ran toward the pine trees by the barn and grain shed, and started a fire at the bottom of the tree. Our dad and Dwaine fought the fire using wet gunny sacks soaked in water and shovels. There was no such device as a garden hose or faucet, just pails of water. They were able to contain the fire fairly quickly and it didn't get into the trees and spread. Normally pine trees will explode and the fire will spread very quickly because they are dried out. Our trees were not dry and they had plenty of moisture in them. They had to keep watch to make sure that it didn't start up again and that it was completely out.

There was another fire that happened on a neighbor's property. It was a big fire, most likely started from lightening. The sky glowed red as all the farmers in the area fought the fire with their barrels of water, gunny sacks, and shovels. Dwaine was not allowed to go and fight this fire; it was too dangerous for him to be out there. There was no fire department to call, so those who lived near a fire had to take care of it themselves.

We had a fire pit between the house and the pine trees in which Judy and Dianne started a fire but it got pretty big; it didn't spread to the trees or pine needles, though. Our dad was able to contain it, but he took their hands and held them over the flames so they would understand how hot fire can be. He didn't burn them, he just made them realize how dangerous it was to play with fire.

Although we knew others had more than we did, we were unaware of the fact that we were not of means. There was always plenty of milk, butter, and food to eat. For about one month in the late winter, we were limited on our milk consumption because the cows were expecting new calves. Milking was reduced until they gave birth. Our dad always kept one cow out of the herd for our table supply but she was usually young and had not yet become a good milk producer.

Bette, Joanne, Dwaine, Dianne on blanket

Dianne

Joanne Pierzina, Dianne, and Bette

Grandma Pierzina with her grandbabies

*Left: Dwaine with cousin Marie Becker, Dianne struggling,
Judy, Bette, Joanne Pierzina in front.*

Grandma Hankes letting the girls feed the chickens
Joanne, Dianne (blond) and Bette in back

Dwaine with his dad

This car was also used as a hauling vehicle. The back seat was removed and it was filled with sacks of chicken feed and brought home. With the seat out, we usually had to sit on our haunches.

51

Dianne fell in a pail of milk

She's not too happy as she cries her wee little heart out. Mom must have been laughing so hard when taking the picture.

Bette

Bette and Dianne

Joanne and Bette at Grandpa and Grandma Hankes's

"Grandpa Go Boom"
One of his favorite sayings when the children fell or got hurt

He sat in a cart that was used to move milk cans. We must have butchered a bunch of chickens, notice all the feathers on the ground.

"Winter in Minnesota"

Dwaine about six years old

Dwaine with team of horses

Winter Wonderland

Dwaine with Shep

56

Our Mom,

Helen

Our Dad,

Alois

Georgie Porgie

Russell and George

With what looks like a broken sled on the wagon.

George is not wearing a skirt, it's a pair of shorts that belonged to his sister and were too big for him.

George and Russell

Looks like a couple of little boys found the girls' dolls.

Dwaine and Bette

Bette still remembers the day this picture was taken because she was so cold, but it's obvious why—her hands are bare, no mittens. Dwaine doesn't look like he's going to share.

Bette driving tractor through deep snow

Dwaine showing that he's better

Caught in the driveway

This is what happens when trying to beat a blizzard home.

Russell, Judy and Dwaine

Shoveling the car out before the snow plow can come through.

George, Russell, and Judy

Standing on bank of snow that has been piled up after shoveling by hand. That was a lot of snow to move.

Snow plow coming through

Looks like they still need shovel help, Daddy in front of plow.

It looks like a second plow can be seen on the road, but that would have been unusual.

It takes a big powerful machine to move that snow

Russell, Judy and Dianne

The driveway has just been plowed as they stand in front of bank.

❧ Chapter Three ❧

Plenty of Work to Do

Dwaine standing in field of freshly mown hay as tall as he is

Horses are in their harnesses, the blinders on each side of the eyes prevented them from spooking easily or being distracted from sights around them–it kept their eyes focused in front of them.

Although we had many hours of leisure time, the farm is not a place that allows you to be lazy for long. When there was work to be done, we all had to pitch in and do our share. Every summer, I'm sure the hottest days were deliberately chosen to bring in the hay. It was stored in the hayloft in the barn as feed for the cows. Our dad would take two girls with him and we would ride on the hay rack being pulled by a team of horses to the field where the hay had recently been cut. He usually used hired hands at that time of year also.

He would lay out two ropes called a sling that extended the length and breadth of the hay rack. The reason he put down the sling was so that he could pile the hay on top of the ropes and they would be the means of getting the hay into the hayloft. When the wagon was half full, a second sling was laid down to be covered over with more hay. Our job was to compress the hay down by stepping on it. The guys on the ground would lift a pitchfork full of hay throwing it onto the wagon and hopefully it missed those of us up there. Often times with four guys doing the throwing, we had to scoot to keep up with them. The dust, chafing, and bugs would get down the necks of our dresses, we always wore a dress and our legs got scratched. It was fun for a while, but soon got tiresome. This was a chore that went on for days. It took many loads of hay to fill that big hayloft and feed all those cows and horses.

Poor quality picture shows Mom on hayrack with Dwaine, Judy, and baby Russell, (Dianne and Bette on ground)
Most likely they stomped down the hay on that day.

When the wagon became full it was driven to the barn and parked beneath the large doors of the hayloft. Each end of the sling was brought together, making a big ball of hay. This was attached to a larger rope that ran up through the large doors and along a track in the ceiling the whole length of the barn. The other end of this large rope went out a small door at the back of the barn to a short post in the ground where a pulley was attached. The rope went through the pulley. A pulley is an apparatus that the rope is fed through, allowing the rope to move with ease as it spins with the movement. The rope is then hooked to the tractor. When the tractor moves forward, it pulls on the rope and lifts the pile or now ball of hay up to the loft, carries it into the loft and released wherever our dad chose. Sometimes they released by themselves and usually made a mess, especially if it wasn't in the loft yet. There was a trip mechanism allowing one end of the rope to fall away. After the tractor moved forward and the hay was released, the rope was unhooked from the tractor, and then Dwaine and Bette would grab the rope, pulling it back behind the pulley. Then the tractor was backed up to the pulley and the rope reattached for a second load. The other end of the rope is pulled back through the barn to the hay rack, so any slack has now been taken up and the rope is now taut again and ready to take another load into the hayloft.

We had a large, wooden, slatted crate used for hauling pigs. When the hay lifting procedure was going on, our parents made all the kids sit in the pig crate for safety. Any number of things could happen; the ropes could snap, the team of horses could bolt and run, or the load could be released prematurely. They always made a head count and double checked again, but only this one day, it didn't happen, much to the regret of our dad who lived with the pain of it for the rest of his life.

Dianne, being only three years old, had gotten behind the pulley area so she could pull the rope back like she's seen the older kids do so many times. This time, the tractor was moving forward lifting a load into the hayloft. The driver, a hired hand, was unaware that Dianne was back there. The rope was large and heavy, she couldn't have pulled it, but she thought she was working. What it did do instead, was it pulled her forward right into the pulley, severely crushing the bones in her right hand. I was only five years old at the time and still vividly remember seeing those pure-white, jagged bones among all the red. I wanted to hold her so bad. While my parents were running to get Lysol and bandages, they let me hold her.

Dianne getting ready to leave for Gillette Children's Hospital where she had already spent three months

Dianne spent three months at Gillette Children's Hospital in St. Paul. Because the accident removed the skin from the top of her hand, the doctors wanted to try a new procedure. They wanted to make new skin to cover her hand. They tried to graft some skin from her leg, but that graft didn't take. Then the doctors turned her hand over so that the top of her hand was against her stomach and she was not able to use or move her hand, it was taped or tied securely in place. When the tape and bandages were removed, she remembers trying to lift her hand up and it was attached to her stomach. Her hand and her stomach were now as one. This procedure was successful and she got new skin for her hand. The bones in her finger were shattered so badly the doctors couldn't repair it, so her pointer finger was never again straight. She was so adept at camouflaging it that most people were unaware that it had been injured.

Dwaine worked as hard as any hired hand we had. He was capable of doing chores that would be unheard of today and was in fact quite rare even in those days. He was only six years old when he was driving the tractor and shortly thereafter was working the fields. Once when he was about fourteen, he was plowing the field and it was beginning to get dark, but he was trying to finish the job. He ran over a pile of old straw that was left over from the previous year and the tractor tipped over. He first felt it teetering and then he knew that it was going to go over, so he jumped as far as he could. He was clear of the tractor when it lay down on the ground. He came into the house white as a sheet and told us what happened. He was more scared to tell us about it than living through it. He was not hurt and the tractor was not damaged, they just tipped it back over with a second John Deere tractor we had.

Dwaine with overturned tractor
On wheel: Dianne, Bette, Judy and Russell.

69

Sitting on straw pile: Russell, Judy, Bette, and Dianne

We all had to learn how to drive the tractor, although we never were as good as Dwaine. For many years, we weren't strong enough to put the tractor in the forward gear, so we held it in place with our foot. The gear was a vertical, long, narrow rod that when pushed forward, made the tractor go forward. If the gear wasn't in position, it went back into the neutral position and the tractor stopped. In the summertime, we put the rod between our toes and kept it going forward. When it became cold and we wore our shoes, our feet kept slipping off and we had a hard time keeping it going.

Great sport for us was hanging onto the back of the trailer while our dad drove using either a team of horses or the tractor because neither went very fast. After riding for a while, we'd jump off and run along behind while hanging on and when we got tired of running, we'd jump back up onto the trailer and ride again.

There were dreaded chores that had to be done every year. Probably the worst was picking rocks in the fields. The rocks had to be picked because you couldn't get a decent crop with a field full of rocks. Rocks will damage the equipment from the plowing, cultivating, planting, to mowing at harvest time. Every spring the earth burped up an incredible amount of rocks. Some of them were big boulders that required the team of horses or tractor to get out. They were forced upward by the freezing cold ground. We picked a wagon full every spring from each field. Our dad was always so full of praise when we could pick up a big one which made us want to please him all the more. He never failed to tell us we did a good job when we did. The rocks then had to be unloaded onto the rock pile that was located next to the cow pasture. This job was done with the team of horses, because the ground was still too soft from the spring thaw for the tractor. The ground could be frozen for as much as six feet down in the winter.

This is what happens when the tractor is driven into soft dirt

One of the fields next to the cow pasture had lain fallow and it was covered with brush. It was decided to plant this field. A very large rock had been found in the field which had been removed but there was another one next to it that was still buried in the ground. Dwaine was clearing this field when the front of the tractor went into the partially filled hole that was created from the first rock and he hit the buried rock so hard it broke the front wheel on the tractor. Dwaine said if it was steel, it just would have bent it but the cast iron shattered. They picked up the pieces and took them into Randall and had them welded back together—which was very hard to weld—but the result was good as new. He's very lucky he wasn't thrown off the tractor, because it had to be a very hard impact to break the wheel.

This same field was being cleared of brush using a dozer and moving all the brush into a large pile for burning. Mom was always finding birds' nests and while she was looking through the pile of brush she found a Thrush's bird nest. It was completely intact with the baby birds still inside even though it had been moved all over the field to make it to the burning pile. She would not let them burn the pile until after the baby birds left their nest.

Using the team of horses, Dwaine was mowing a field of hay with the mower and noticed that one of the blades on the sickle broke off. Even though he knew it was gone, he did not stop to replace it but continued with the mowing. When our dad returned home he saw the four inch or so strips of hay all over the field that was not mowed but was still standing. After he had a talk with Dwaine about that, Dwaine never did that again. For a while Dwaine thought he was going to be made to cut the strips of hay by hand with a scythe. It was considered an embarrassment for a farmer to have that in his field.

I was about seven years old when we did another dreaded chore, which was picking the corn. The corn had to go through a freeze before it could be picked, and by then the weather was getting cold, very cold. We had to break the corn cob away from the stalks and remove the husks, which is the outer covering protecting the ear of corn. Our dad devised a hook that he attached to his wrist and hand and slid it down the length of the ear of corn and automatically removed the husk exposing the ear and making it easier to break it away from the stalk, so he could work a little faster than the others. The ears of corn were then thrown on the wagon, which had one side boarded so the corn wouldn't go over the other side and onto the ground. This job required one of us to drive the tractor at a slow pace, moving only as fast as the men worked with hand picking. When you're on the ground, you can stay a little warm by just moving around. When you're doing the driving you're sitting in the open because there's no covering or shelter, so we got very cold. We did have to wear our shoes, so we were constantly trying to keep the tractor going as our shoes kept slipping off the rod. Driving the tractor usually fell on one of the three girls.

After the corn cobs were picked, they were taken to the corn crib and shoveled in. That made the crows and squirrels very happy because they were small enough to fit inside the corn crib. Russell and George were in the corn crib when some squirrels were eating the corn. Russell tried to feed one but the squirrel bit him instead. Dianne caught a baby squirrel and still carries the scar on her hand from that incident. Generally they won't let you near them, so getting that close was a rarity

The corn stalks were left standing and the cows were turned loose in the field for a couple of days and cleaned up what they would eat which were only the leaves, they didn't eat the stalks, which were dried out and had no nourishment. The stalks were left standing and in the spring of the following year, they were plowed under.

We had a tool that was called a scythe, which had a long sharp curved blade and a very long handle. The handle was longer than I was tall, so it was a little hard for me to handle. Dianne and I thought we'd do our dad a favor and cut the whole corn field down for him. We could just imagine how happy he would be. We got the scythe and while she was holding the stalk for me, I tried cutting it off. It seems that my aim wasn't very good because instead of cutting the corn stalk, I cut her right across her hand; lucky for us it was dull so the cut wasn't as bad as it could have been if it had been sharpened. Instead of the praise and glory we envisioned, I got a spanking for that, but I already felt sorry for what I did.

After the silo was built, the corn that went into the silo was processed differently. That corn was harvested earlier in the year, making it younger, moist and with more nourishment. A machine would cut the corn stalks at ground level and with binder twine it would automatically tie several stalks into bundles and the bundles would fall to the ground. Then the men walked through the fields and stacked the bundles, similar to a small teepee. This made it easy to then come along with a wagon and throw them on. If they happened to run out of the twine then they had to go along later and tie them by hand and that was quite a chore. The wagon of corn cobs and stalks were then taken to the barn area and run through a chipper, grinding it up and then blown into the silo and it was called silage which was a real treat for the cows and it was good for them. In the winter the silage was frozen solid, so it had to be chipped away with a pick and was not easy to get out. Not to mention that the silo itself was very cold, like working in a freezer.

We lived on two-hundred-and-sixty-five acres plus sixty-five acres that was added a few years later and all the land that could be utilized was put to use, so more than one field of corn was planted. The old cold method still had to be done because that corn was needed for other feedings. Some of the ears were taken to the grain shed and put through the grinder making ground feed for some of the animals. The pigs were fed whole ears but they only ate the kernels, they didn't eat the cob and the cobs became part of their bedding along with straw. If we wanted to feed the geese and chickens, we removed the corn from the cobs. This meant taking the corn and with our hands wringing or twisting the kernels away from the cob. Most of the time it came off easy but the kernels were hard and sharp, so it was painful on the hands. Gloves were not in great supply at our home.

Potato Digger

Another dreaded chore we had was to pick potatoes. This one was the easiest because it was generally done in one day, where the others went on for several days. After our dad planted the potatoes and the plants withered on the vine it was time to dig them up from underground. This implement was called a potato digger. It was hooked to the tractor or the team of horses. The front of this equipment would dig down into the ground and the vines along with the dirt and potatoes would move up the machine on a conveyer belt that vibrated away the vines and dirt, leaving only the potatoes to move up and over the top and drop to the ground behind it. We walked along behind it and picked up the potatoes putting them into buckets and then dumped them into gunny sacks and they were left in the field to be picked up and put on a wagon by the men.

The potatoes were then taken to the house and put in the spooky ole basement where they were handy to get a bucketful whenever we needed them. They lasted all winter and longer without spoiling and they were a major part of our food supply.

The potatoes that were not eaten by the time planting season came around again the following spring were used as the seeds. On each potato there are kind of notches called eyes, where a root will sprout if the potato gets old. One potato is cut into many pieces, but there must always be an eye in the piece that will get planted. You may get as many as ten eyes on one potato, and each will bear a plant. If there is no eye on the piece of potato planted, it will simply rot in the ground.

Dwaine remembers when he was with our dad in the field as he was cultivating a potato crop and a rabbit was running up one row and down the other with our dog chasing it. Our dad thought it would make a tasty dish for supper, so he decided to try to catch it. Leaving the team of horses standing, he stooped down low to grab it as it ran by. The rabbit still running from the dog ran right into our dad as our dad made a lunge for it, and the dog did the same, all three colliding. After the dust settled, it seems that our dad got the short end of it. No rabbit for supper, our dad was dusty, dirty and bleeding pretty bad. The dog didn't get his rabbit and the rabbit got away.

In the very early years that we lived on the farm, we grew a really huge cucumber garden. Dwaine was big enough to go out every day and pick them with our dad and he wasn't very crazy about picking the prickly things. They would start at row one and go up and down each row. Dwaine was always so glad to see the end of the rows because he knew they were finished, only to start all over again the next day on row one because the plants continued to produce. He was sure glad when they stopped reproducing and that was the only year that we raised cucumbers. It seems there was a lot of hand work and involved many hours, so it wasn't very profitable. He remembers going to Bowlus which was quite a distance away from Randall to sell them. There was a co-op that would buy them and most likely they ended up going to the cannery and becoming dill pickles. These trips were made after supper and the other chores were done, because they couldn't afford to waste daylight hours.

Along with farm chores there were house chores, too; namely, washing clothes. We had a gasoline-powered, wringer washing machine. It was loud and noisy but was far better than the scrub board. Normally this was set up on the porch, but in the bitterest weather, it had to be done inside the house. This was an all day job that had to be done at least once a week with six grubby kids and not a lot of clothing that would last much longer. Large containers had to be filled with water and heated on the stove, then carried to the washing machine.

Sometimes Mom made her own soap, two ingredients she used was lye and rendered lard and these were formed into hard blocks. When we bought laundry soap it was called Fels Naptha which was also formed in hard blocks, but not quite as hard as the homemade soap. I had the chore of cutting it into small pieces with a knife and they both were as hard as a rock.

White clothes were washed first in very hot, soapy water. After the load agitated and clothing was clean, we used a stick to get the clothes out because the water was too hot to put our hands in. Then we had to handle the hot fabric to put them through the wringer. The wringer had two long rubber rollers that squeezed all the water out and back into the washing machine while the clothes dropped into a wash tub of warm rinse water. One always had to

pay attention to how the clothes were fed through the rollers because a shirt could lose its entire row of buttons unless they were safely folded inside the fabric, making sure that they were lying flat. If you weren't paying attention, you could get your hand caught causing injury. There was a release on it that opened the jaws, but it was better if you were more careful and only let your fingertips get close, but not too close.

Wringer washer

The wringer was attached to the washer by a post on the left side making it moveable, able to make a full circle where it would swing around until it was in a position of choice and then locked into place. Turning it a quarter circle, and then locking it enabled us to put the clothing from the first rinse through the wringer squeezing all the water out again and dropping into a second rinse tub. Then moving the wringer another quarter turn, the second rinsed clothing was dropped into a wicker laundry basket and taken to the clothesline and hung to dry.

The same water was used beginning with the white clothes and continued with darker colors until the men's work clothes were finished. More water was added as it was needed but by the time the wash day ended the water was pretty dark and thick.

Outerwear was separated and put in a tub of starch solution, wrung out, and then hung to dry. After the starched clothes were dry, we sprinkled them down with water, using a bottle with holes punched in the lid, rolled them up tight, then covered the basket with a sheet and allowed them to absorb the moisture for about a day, and then we ironed them. I remember one time when our dad's boxer shorts accidently got starched and ironed. He was not too happy!

All clothing was ironed including our dad's underwear, pillow cases, and handkerchiefs because the fabric was 100% cotton and got very wrinkled. Before we got electricity, the iron was heated on the cook stove. There were about four irons with one handle, allowing you to change irons often. While one was being used, the other three were getting hot. I remember Mom would put the iron on a white shirt, only to find the iron was too hot and a perfect imprint of the iron was on the shirt. I rarely ironed with the old heavy iron but after we got electricity, for the most part, the ironing became my job with the new electric iron that was also very heavy.

In the winter the subzero weather was so cold that when you hung clothes on the clothes line they froze solid, known as freeze dry. Your bare hands froze too because you couldn't wear gloves or mittens to hang the clothes. After they were brought into the house, they were spread out to dry on a portable clothes rack. Somehow they were almost dry when they thawed out.

This image of the washing machine is similar to what we used. After we got electricity we got another wringer washing machine that looked like the old one but was much better, we just plugged it into the socket and we didn't have to pump the water and heat it on the stove because hot water now came out of the kitchen faucet.

The first picture showing our dad sharpening the blades to the mower was taken beside the barn and this was before the milk room had been built. Visible in the picture above dad's shoulders is the pump for water which is in the location of what will be the holding tank for the icy water where we kept the milk after the milking is done. Running along the barn is a pipe that piped water into a tank that held the water for the cows while they were in the cow pen in back.

Our dad sharpening the blades with the grinding stone
Dwaine, Dianne, and Bette watching

Picture was taken beside the barn, but normally this job is done in the building that collapsed.

A Mower

The blades that are being sharpened will be attached to this equipment, which lays low to the ground. The high grass would make it very difficult to see a child or animal that happened to be in the field, so we were not allowed to be anywhere nearby when the mowing was being done.

A Threshing Machine

Brought into the field to harvest the oats. The oat kernels were separated and went into a gunny sack attached to the machine. The straw goes out the tall shoot, as can be seen on right, and becomes bedding for the animals. At one time our grandfather George Pierzina owned such a machine and traveled the countryside doing this work. He was only about seventeen years old then.

Oats being conveyed into hayloft into special bin built for oats

Dwaine remembers that this was only done in early years; after that, it was put in gunny sacks and carried to the loft.

Dwaine with pigs

They scavenge for leftover oats that had fallen to the ground—little is wasted on the farm.

81

Dwaine riding with Dad

Going alongside a field of planted corn.

Judy fell asleep on the job

Even at an early age we learned the names of each tool that our dad had or would need and the difference between an eight penny nail and a sixteen penny nail. We were his little legs to run to the tool room in the barn and retrieve it for him.

Georgie and Russell

Learning from their dad who was always the teacher.

Must have gotten it fixed

Shep looks like he has a smile on his face as he's looking for a little petting or attention.

Digging foundation for silo

Dwaine on left in trench, George, Judy, Russell, and Dad on right.

Getting it off the ground

You can see the cement tiles that will be put in place as it goes up.

Our dad helping the contractor as he builds the silo

Looks like Russell wearing oversized working gloves must be a big help.

The silo is finished now and has a coat of white paint

The upper squares are black and white checkers.

A field of corn in background and a load of corn stalks on the wagon, getting ready to put into silo. Note the area between the silo and the barn; this is the chute and ladder to get into and also to fill the silo. The silage is later thrown down the chute and taken into the barn to feed the cows.

The ladder to get to the top of the silo is on the other side and not visible from this angle.

These rocks were removed from the field

We pulled out big rocks every year.

Judy, George, and Dwaine did the work...plus, two tractors and the dog.

Our dad with his sister and brother. Aunt Ione with Uncle Geo's friend from CA, Uncle George behind Dwaine

Our dad is wearing his usual working clothing, his bib overalls.

❧ *Chapter Four* ❧

Our Country School

District #49

Bell located in the steeple at back end of roof. Boy's outhouse in back.

W e attended a one-room country school called District #49, with classes ranging from grades one through eight. At the front door, we entered into an area where we hung our coats, removed our rubbers in the winter, and kept our lunch pails.

Along the side of the entry was a flag pole where we flew the flag, but only on special days. The teacher rang the school bell every morning. She did this by pulling on a rope that was attached to the bell and hung down through the ceiling at the front of the classroom. Anyone arriving after the bell rang was considered tardy. We started every morning with the Pledge of Allegiance and a prayer.

Our subjects were what they called the three R's, Reading, Riting & Rithmatic, and all the basics such as history and geography plus music, art, penmanship, etc.

Entire school (minus five)

Dwaine is in back row, 1st boy from right. Dale Nelson, face partially hidden 3rd boy from right. Judy, Dianne, and Bette in front row on left.

Our desks were aligned in a row on strips of wood, with about six desks per strip and there were four rows, accommodating about twenty-four students. You couldn't move your desk without moving all the desks attached to the strips of wood they were secured to. The desk top lifted up and we kept our books and papers in there. Each desk had an ink well in the top corner. These ink wells were rarely used, if at all. We all used wooden pencils for our work and we did have a pencil sharpener that we operated by turning a crank handle. Work was also done on the blackboard in front of the classroom.

A fairly small wood burning stove heated the school. It had a protective sheeting going around it so no student could accidently get burned unless they went to the inside of the sheeting and touched the stove. When Dwaine got older he was usually in charge of building the fire in the morning. Our last teacher was getting old, so she relied on him to do that. She gave us the keys to the building because we usually got there before her unless we found something of interest to catch our attention like critters or a giant ant hill.

Outside at the back of the school were two outhouses, one for the boys and one for the girls. Every Halloween, without fail, some of the older boys from town would turn them over during the night. It was pretty easy access for them because the school was located right on Highway 115 and the outhouses were close to the road.

There was no running water; in fact there was no water. There was a pump in the school yard, but it didn't work, the well may have run dry. In the morning, two students were allowed to go to the creek and fill a bucket of water. They went across the highway and down a hill where there was a spring that produced underground very good clean drinking water. They were each paid $1 a month for their work. Two different students were chosen each month so it was rotated among the bigger kids. The bucket of water was set on a low bench alongside a pan of water where we washed our hands with a bar of soap that we all shared. There was a ladle placed in the water bucket and all the students shared the drinking water using the same ladle. One can only imagine the germs that were spread.

School started in first grade, there was no kindergarten. The number of students didn't change very much and it always stayed pretty consistent. Those that graduated were replaced by younger ones. We didn't know of any family that moved away. Dwaine's class had three students, Bette had two, Dianne had two, Judy had three, Russell had four, and George never attended the little school.

I would like to say that I was the smartest kid in my grade but that only means that I was smarter than Edward Waltman because all through school there were only two of us. I know I was smarter than him because I could count to 100 before he could.

As a student, we could learn from the advanced classes, because the teacher taught the students in front of the whole school. A fifth grader could learn a lot by listening to the eighth graders lessons. All the students took part in the Spelling Bees, which we had about once a week. The whole student body was divided into two teams and lined up against the walls. The first graders spelled words from their spelling books, as did each grade, right up to the eighth graders.

We put on plays and skits at school that were always fun to organize. The kids were all allowed to join in and make decisions. We always decorated the school with whatever theme or holiday was current. In the fall of the year, we would go into the woods and learn the different trees and bring leaves back to the classroom and turn them into decorations.

Recess was something we looked forward to and we all played together. We played baseball, dodge ball, Annie over the Woodshed and many other games that everybody took part in. After recess and lunch were over, the teacher rang the bell and we'd all come running, although none of us left the school yard. A wire fence encircled the school except at the highway.

We never had homework; we did our work at school only. All the children had a long walk to and from school and it was a rare treat to get a ride. Many of the students lived on a farm so there wasn't time to do homework; farm chores had to be done. Before Dwaine could leave for school the cows had to be milked and fed. In the warmer days, they had to be taken to the cow pasture to graze all day.

In early days we carried a tin pail for our lunch box; it measured about eight inches high and had a handle and a lid. It was a lard container before we made it our lunch pail. When we were lucky enough to get paper bags, we used them too. We liked the sacks better because we didn't have to carry them home, we could put them in our pocket. Our lunch was usually a peanut butter and jelly sandwich wrapped in wax paper, cookies and fruit, most often an apple.

We walked about three miles every day, each way. We rarely walked the way of the road, but cut through our field, the sheep pasture, John O. Johnson's field, and a path through the woods. The path was a road that was made by an early settler. There was a small abandoned log house and the old road had not grown over with trees which made easier walking. Sometimes we walked the highway but it was a much longer walk. Although the highway was farther, it could be easier walking because in the winter the snow plow went through the night before and cleared the high snow away.

We had the longest walk of all the students because our farm was the furthest from school. We lived right on the border line to attend District #49 or attend a school near Randall. Either choice would have been about the same distance except there were no shortcuts if the Randall school had been chosen. It would have been county road and highway all the way, not nearly as interesting as what the fields and river had to offer.

For the first two years, while being a first and second grader, Dwaine walked this distance by himself. He said that after getting to school, the older girls would hug up on him and everybody was so nice and kind to him. It seems unbelievable that that little boy traveled this route alone in summer and winter. There was nothing between our farm and the school except for a vast amount of land, woods and the Johnson farm and he said that the Johnson's often brought him in and warmed him up before setting him on his way again. He said that Mom often came through the field to meet him and help him the rest of the way home.

To get to school, we crossed our field, then through the sheep pasture and then on the county road and over the bridge and walking a short distance further we entered onto a roadway that led to the Johnson farm. Before reaching their farm, to the right of the roadway was a hill and on the other side of the hill was another farm which sat below the hill that was not visible from this road. This farm was owned by a man named Fred. They had a large yellow dog that was having great sport by lying in wait and chasing Dwaine and I as we walked down the road. One day while walking home from school this dog bit Dwaine on the wrist. He says that he was between the dog and me because he was protecting his little sister. When we got home our dad took his gun and went to Fred's farm and gave him the choice to either shoot his dog himself or he's going to do it. Fred said he would do it and he did, so we were never bothered by their dog again.

A very nice older couple lived on the John O. Johnson farm. Mr. Johnson was a portly man who was always smiling. He always reminded me of the man in the moon. He would stop his busy work to wave to us and did this until we were out of sight. Often Mrs. Johnson would take us into her house and warm us up in front of her oven before we set off again. Her daughters were grown and no longer living at home and one day she gave me a very large doll that I was just thrilled with. I only had the doll about a week when I came home from school and found that my sisters or brothers smashed a hole in the dolls forehead. About a week after that, Mrs. Johnson stopped me because she made several dresses for the doll. I told her what happened to the doll but she made me take the clothes anyway.

In the winter we had to contend with snow but in the summer it was sand burs. Wherever we walked there were weeds that were loaded with sand burs which were sharp, spiny burs that were painful and difficult to remove from clothing. Our socks and shoelaces would be covered with burs. This weed grows in the spring and will continue to grow until the first hard frost or freeze occurs in the fall, so we had to deal with them the whole summer but then here comes winter. Which could be worse?

One day Dwaine, a third grader and an older neighbor boy Dale Nelson and I were walking home from school. It was a nice warm September day with lots of dry grass. We were at the edge of the woods when Dale showed Dwaine some matches he had so they started building little fires, which they stomped out right away. I was scared and crying and telling them not to do it, but they ignored me and kept making more fires. They let one get too big for them to stomp out and before we knew it, there was a big fire. I was scared out of my wits and took off running for home leaving Dwaine and Dale behind. I didn't know a six-year-old could run so fast. Once in a while I looked back over my shoulder and saw the huge black smoke and flames, which only made me run faster just wanting to get to the safety of home. My side was hurting so bad but I didn't stop, I just kept running. I made it into the house, jumped on the couch and looked out the window and saw the entire east was filled with thick black smoke. I'm not sure which was worse, my side hurting so bad because I could hardly move or the horrors of seeing all the smoke. The farmers and local residents including our dad fought that fire all night long. The grass in the school yard was burned and they barely saved the school, but the entire woods were all lost. I was of legal age before our parents ever found out that we had anything to do with that fire. I say "we," but I never touched a match.

Our dad was on the school board and in charge of District #49. He took care of the finances and paid the bills including issuing the checks for the teacher's salary and the students who were the water kids for the month. The teacher would tell him what supplies were needed and he would fill the order for her.

I loved first grade and we had such a wonderful teacher. I was hungry to learn and school was such a joy every day. Things changed for us when I turned seven years old and entered into the second grade and Dwaine was nine years old in the fourth grade.

We got a new teacher. She disliked having to ask our dad for things that were needed and felt that she should be able to order supplies and take care of the operation of the school herself without going through him. She was a sister-in-law to our aunt and we overheard a conversation between our parents to that effect. Our dad could be on the frugal and practical side and maybe he didn't allow her something she may have wanted.

I can only say that she made school a living hell for Dwaine and me. Every day was torture, ridicule, embarrassment, and humiliation that she directed at us at every opportunity. She'd walk up and down the rows of desks with a ruler and she'd hit us with it, mostly on the hands or the head or it might be the book we were reading—and always without a reason. Sometimes being hit with the ruler was easier to take than her humiliation. Dwaine bore the treatment like a young man but I put my head on my desk and cried. Every day, I seemed to be crying in school.

The teacher made me get up in front of the class to read from my Dick and Jane reader. I was only in the second grade and hadn't learned to put letters together yet and before I had a chance to sound them out, she barked out what the word was. She never gave me a chance to read and got disgusted telling me to go sit down, which was so humiliating because I knew I could do it.

She also sent me to the blackboard to do some arithmetic problems that she had written. It seems I was too slow for her because I was using my fingers to find the total, and she angrily took the chalk from my hand and wrote the answer. My eyes were full of tears and I could no longer see the blackboard, there didn't seem to be anything that I could do to please her.

I worked real hard learning to put my letters together so I could read them quickly but when I was sent back up to the front of the room, the words didn't come out, they were stuck in my throat. Every day was a mirror of the day before and a continuation of the days to come.

Dwaine and I were the only students who got this treatment from her. The rest of the students were spared her anger, hate, or whatever was driving her. Her daughter attended the same school but only because her mother was the teacher. Not only was Dwaine subjected to the wrath of the mother but also the daughter who harbored the same vengeance. One day the daughter dug her fingernails in Dwaine's face, making a deep wound across the bridge of his nose and downward and he still carries the scar from that. It bled profusely and he got in trouble—but she got off scot-free.

We were no match for this bitter, middle-aged, sharp tongued, ruler-wielding woman. We never told our parents what was happening in school. I'm not sure if it was because we didn't question authority, or if it was because she was related to our aunt.

Our dad—who never used anything but his hand for discipline on our backside—would not have taken kindly to what was going on in the classroom, and especially the fact that we were being hit with a ruler. He always praised us for the little accomplishments we achieved and he would have been appalled at the angry, sharp tone of voice that she used on us. One can now only imagine the anger that our dad would have unleashed on her and consequences be damned. It was a wonderful year when she was replaced the following year with an elderly teacher who was kind, but the scars lived on.

The farm next to ours became vacant and was vacant for several months. It was a big two-story house. Dwaine and I were walking home from school one day, I would have been in the second grade and he in the fourth grade, and we thought it didn't belong to anyone anymore because nobody was living in it. There were no locks on the doors then, even on vacant houses. We went into the house and started breaking the windows. Oh what fun we had! We didn't stop until every window was broken. I have no clue why we did this, but once we started, we didn't stop until both stories—upstairs and downstairs—were done. Daddy didn't even ask if we did it, he knew without asking. We both got a darn good whupping, big red handprints on the backside for some time. Our dad had to pay for our misdeed and most likely do the repair work, too. He took Dwaine to the township dump and told him if he wanted to break glass he can come to the dump and break all the glass he wants to. Many years later, our cousin, Tom Pierzina, the same Tom that was afraid of the bull, and his wife Carolyn bought this same house.

Mom always had a way of putting magic in everything. When the leaves on the trees started turning colors in the fall, she told us that Jack Frost comes in the night and paints them. On our way to school, walking down the Johnson road with trees on both sides of the road, it would be full of color, every day more and more was added to the trees. We envisioned the little leprechaun Jack Frost out with his magic paint brush creating all the vivid colors for us to enjoy and we appreciated how hard he must have worked. We didn't realize that it was part of Mother Nature.

We listened to the school closures on the battery powered radio which always brought out a chorus of "yippee" if District #49 was named. If our school was closed, so were all the others. In the event the teacher couldn't make it to school for whatever reason, then that would be announced too, it didn't happen often but it did happen. Weather predictions were not very good; technology just wasn't there yet. A blizzard could come in and catch everyone by surprise. We were instructed that if this happened while we were in school, we were to stay in school and not try to come home. We were to build a fire in the stove and spend the night if it were necessary. We may go hungry but at least we could stay warm and not freeze to death out in the elements.

Minnesota gets fiercely cold in the winter. From December through February, the temperature would be around zero-to-minus zero. By March it would creep up to maybe 10 to 30 degrees, which is still very cold. The wind could be biting cold as we walked across the open fields and there was no protection against that. We wore a scarf across our mouths but by the time we got to school or home, it was just frozen ice across our faces, caused by our breath.

We never wore a pair of pants to school, we only wore dresses. To help stay warmer in the winter we wore thermal long johns that came to the waist line, not full body. We wore these with long stockings over them. We thought all long johns were the same, an opening in the back for the girls and an opening in front for the boys. I was in the outhouse with another girl and I saw there was a difference. Hers was made for girls with no slits at all. That's when I realized I was wearing my brother's hand-me-downs!! I was embarrassed and I didn't want her to see my openings. A few years later we wore pants under our dresses but that was only in the winter time. Dianne rarely wore pants and she probably never wore the long johns, either. If it was really cold, she'd put the pants on for a while, but always took them off a short time later. She was such a girly girl, always has been and still is.

Our coats were just ordinary coats, usually made of wool. We wore overshoes which were only a pair of rubbers that we slipped on over our shoes. There wasn't any lining or fur in them so we didn't derive any warmth, just protection from getting our feet wet. Hmmm, so why did we always have wet shoes? Our mittens were made of cotton, which always got wet. We rarely got a pair of gloves because our parents felt that with mittens, we could curl our hands up inside and keep them warmer. Even with the mittens we had, our hands would get so cold, just freezing, where they just hurt so badly. Mom would make us put our hands in cold water to thaw them out. It seems logical to put them in warm water but that would make them hurt so much more, so cold water was the best choice.

When the snow was fresh and deep, it was hard walking because our feet and legs went deep in the snow. Dwaine usually went first in line and made it easier for the rest of us to follow. If the sun had a chance to shine on the snow, it made a thin sheet of ice and we were able to walk on top the snow. But often times, our foot would go through the crust and you had to get your entire leg out of the hole that was just created and most often ended up with lots of snow in our overshoes or rubbers as they were called.

The snow was high on the ground and our dad was taking Dwaine and Bette to school in the sleigh, which is a one-horse-drawn snow vehicle. It was a smooth ride while we were on the road and then we rode through the Johnson driveway to cut across their field. It became pretty hard going as the soft snow in the field got deeper. The runners were too narrow to stay on top of the snow and the sleigh began plowing through the snow. When the snow got high enough to reach the horse's belly, the horse decided he had enough. He bucked and kicked and broke loose from the sleigh and headed back home leaving us stranded in the field. Dwaine and I continued on to school by foot and our dad walked home to get the horse so he could go back and get the sleigh. He and the sleigh were there to pick us up after school let out. The animals always knew their way home.

In the winter, before leaving for school, Mom always sent a quart of freshly made chocolate milk so we would have something warm in us. This jar was put in a pan of water and placed on the wood burning stove at school to heat and we drank it with our sandwiches. One day our teacher accidently broke our jar of chocolate so she offered to bring us another one the next day. We learned quickly that our mother was a much better cook than she was because it was awful. I'm not sure how you can ruin chocolate milk, but she did.

A special treat often waited for us, especially when we came home from school in the cold. Mom always had bread dough mixed up and she would make bread patties from the raw dough and fry them up. That was just so delicious and that would tide us over until supper time.

The farm that suffered our broken windows was eventually bought by a family with six boys who were all younger than us. We walked home from school with them almost every day and a couple of them would usually wet themselves which made the seat of their pants wet. We made them sit on the snow bank while we watched the snow turn blue from the dye in their jeans. One day their father came along and asked us if we wanted a ride. We never turned down a ride, so we jumped in the car. He gave us heck and told us that we were never to do that to his kids again, and then he made us get out of the car. Because he was driving on the road, we had a much longer walk home and we had to go right past their house to get to ours. We never did make them sit on the snow bank or anywhere else again.

In Minnesota the weather can change in a heartbeat. I remember one early fall day, it was warm and sunny as we left for school in the morning. We didn't wear our heavy coats, or snowshoes; there was no need for either as the day was nice. Just before school let out it started to snow. The temperature had to have dropped to the low 30's by three o'clock in the afternoon because it can't snow if it's warmer than that, it would be rain or sleet. The first snowfall of the year was always greeted with excitement and joy, at least for the kids. It was so much fun when we were first in it playing around, but by the time we got home we were so cold. We would have been cold, but still fine if we hadn't dawdled along the way.

Another day a fierce unexpected blizzard came in while we were in school. Our father and our neighbor Monnie Nelson, Dale Nelson, the fire starter's dad, came to school with a team of horses harnessed to a wagon with runners. They were wagon skis that ran on top of the snow without digging in like wheels would have. Loaded on the wagon was a tarp covering a pile of hay and blankets, which we crawled under to stay warm. We were warm and protected, but our dad and Monnie had to sit in the open wagon with strong winds blowing, picking up snow from the ground, similar to what a sand storm would be like but it was icy snow particles instead of sand, hitting their faces with stinging force and also creating big snow drifts. The day turned dark and visibility was next-to-none. We made it to the Nelson's farm which was half way home, where Mrs. Nelson had hot chocolate and a warm oven ready for us. When Daddy and Monnie came into the house, their faces and cheeks were covered with solid sheets of ice and they looked so cold. I don't remember the rest of the trip home, but we left shortly because the roads were completely impassable and the only vehicles that could possibly make it were those with horses. It's very possible that the horses were given their head to find their way home because our dad was not able to see very well without protection for his eyes or for any distance. It is known that many times a farmer cannot find the way back to his house from the barn during a blizzard because you can't see more than a few feet.

Spring was such a welcome time for us. We had high snow banks and lots of snow on the ground but when it all started to thaw, there was water trickling out from under the banks and the running water made almost a musical sound. It was so refreshing and so clean and so much fun to play in. Shoots of plants burst forth even under the snow banks and we knew that it wouldn't be long and the snow would all be gone.

Every spring during the spring thaw, the Little Elk River would overflow and cover the road. It was only then that we were indulged in a ride to the bridge on our way to school. Our early car was a 1932 Chevy, which still ran and was used around the farm for a number of years and sat high up off the ground, but our later cars didn't sit quite so high. The water would come up to the running boards and sometimes into the car because it got so high. I remember one time when Daddy drove us through the water on the tractor and we grabbed a hold wherever we could but that was before there were five us riding. The tractor had only one seat and that was for the driver, our Dad. That didn't work so good for the return trip because we still had to get over the water, so somebody had to be there to meet us. It was then decided that Dwaine would drive the tractor with a trailer attached through the water and then park the tractor and trailer on the other side of the bridge and we walked the rest of the way to school and it was still sitting there waiting for us at the end of the day. We were not allowed to take the tractor all the way to school and we didn't. I make it sound like we never got a ride to or home from school. That's not the case. Anytime Mom or Daddy were out, they timed it so they could pick us up. There just weren't a lot of trips taken.

When crossing the bridge to go to school we stepped lightly and were very quiet because we believed that a sleeping troll was living under the bridge. If we woke him up, he would demand money from us and we didn't have any money or anything else to offer him except our lunch sack and then we'd go hungry, so we couldn't take a chance of waking him. We never saw him but that didn't mean he wasn't there.

In the sheep pasture there were lots of frogs to catch. After the frogs were caught, we'd insert a hollow reed in their rears and blow on it. This put air in their bodies, and then, standing on the bridge we'd throw them into the river and watch them try to dive.

They never could get under water to safety. We could now laugh and giggle and make more noise because if the troll were to come out from under the bridge, we had a nice fat frog to offer him. I'd like to think that we didn't seriously hurt them and hope they didn't have anything more serious than a case of gas for the remainder of the day. Although we dawdled along the way, we scooted along pretty fast after that so we wouldn't be late for school.

From the river bank, we would often catch a snapping turtle and carry it home for Grandpa Hankes. Grandma would make turtle soup from it after Grandpa cleaned it. We had to be very careful that they didn't clamp their jaws down on our hands because once their jaws locked, they couldn't be released. Although we were never allowed to be near the river, we did sometimes manage to be on the banks of the river but never into the water. The river water was different than being in lake water. Lake water was predictable and consistent but river water was constantly moving and changing. The constant, moving current would change the bottom or floor of the riverbed. One day it may be high ground but the next day that same spot could be a deep hole and vice-versa.

When Dwaine was in the fifth grade he got a new bicycle that he rode to school. Dianne had now started first grade so she and I could walk together. With the bicycle he could get home faster than walking and get more chores done earlier. After arriving at school with his bicycle he would park it, there were no bicycle racks or locks and may not have been invented yet. He was the only student with a bicycle so it was a novelty for all of them. An older, much larger eighth grade boy who had cerebral palsy would take the bicycle—which was too small for him—and ride it around but he had no balancing abilities. He had a hard time walking straight because he would drag one leg, much less ride a bicycle and was always riding into things, doing damage, including bending the handlebars. He didn't have the mental capacity to know what he was doing or learn how to ride or understand the word 'no.' He made a beeline for the bicycle every chance he got. One day he fell over with the bicycle and bent the pedal where Dwaine couldn't ride it home but had to push it all the way. After getting home, our dad was able to fix the bent pedal. Dwaine asked the teacher for help to make the boy leave the bicycle alone but it didn't do any good and this continued for quite some time so his bicycle got banged up pretty bad and he didn't even do it.

Death touched us at an early age. One of our fellow students named Bruce was in the sixth grade in Dwaine's class. He and his brother were home alone and messing around with a shotgun that was in the home. The gun went off and Bruce was struck with a single shot in the abdomen causing fatal injuries. It was a very sad time because he was a nice boy. Dwaine and Dale Nelson were two of the pallbearers.

Our shoes were often ordered from the catalog. To make sure we were getting the proper size, Mom would have us step on a sheet of paper and with a pencil she would draw the outline of our foot and send that in along with the order. Getting a new pair of shoes was a special treat and only happened at the beginning of the school year and they had to last the whole year. I was so proud of my new oxfords and it was also the very first day of school. We started walking home and decided to walk the highway rather than going through the woods. As I was walking, I began to scrape the toe of my shoe on the pavement. Before I got home, the soles of my new shoes were flapping and I had to carry them. My brand new shoes were in pretty bad shape. I couldn't walk with the soles flapping with every step, so I put a rubber canning jar ring around the front of my shoes to hold the flap in place. I wore them like that for several days before they were taken to the shoemaker and got them stitched again.

When walking by way of the highway, we had the opportunity to treat ourselves to some gum. After the road had been freshly tarred, we would dig the tar out of the road and pretend we were chewing Black Jack gum. One day a delivery truck lost control of his van and lost dozens of boxes of chocolate candy which were scattered all over in the ditch. With happy smiles on our faces we grabbed armloads of boxes and it was an exciting walk home.

Our parents purchased another sixty-five acres of land between the school and our farm. One day while Dianne and I were walking home from school, she wanted to go visit our dad because he was working on the land. I didn't want to do that, I just wanted to go home and I wanted her to go with me. She went on to the field and I was feeling a little ticked as I walked on alone. I got great satisfaction when I could pull one over on the other kids. I also prided myself a little with my drawings, so I started drawing footprints in the dirt road with a stick, knowing that Diane would be following along shortly. I made great big footprints that measured at least two feet long. I wanted her to think it was a monster. When she got home, she told me about these monster footprints she saw in the road and how they scared her.

A new neighbor boy, also named Dale, not Dale Nelson who was now in the tenth grade, was showing us his cap gun while we were walking home from school. Dwaine was in the eighth grade at the time. Dale put the gun to Dwaine's ear and pulled the trigger. From that day on, Dwaine had impaired hearing in that ear.

The end of the school year was always exciting. We had a big picnic and all the families gathered. What I remember most of all was the ice cream! It was served from large metal containers. We were able to play with other sisters and brothers that we didn't normally see, mainly because they were small children. I was playing on the teeter-totter with a mentally challenged sister of a classmate who didn't attend school. The school had a very long teeter-totter that put you way high in the air. She weighed more than I did, so I had a hard time trying to make this teeter-totter business work. I had to sit at the very end of the board to try to get myself down and her up in the air. She must have gotten tired of the game because when her end was on the ground, she got off leaving me at the highest point that could be reached and I came down with a crash. I hit the ground so hard it knocked the wind out of me and made me nauseous for quite some time.

Dwaine graduated from the eighth grade and would be going to high school as a freshman and that same year I reached seventh grade and we both were transferred to the Little Falls High School. All of the other seventh and eighth graders in the country schools were also transferred. By this time Dale Nelson was already in high school and had his own car, so our parents paid him $1.00 a week to take us to and from school.

The new school in Little Falls offered a hot lunch every day which was something new for us. Dwaine and I both worked in the cafeteria and received our lunches for free. We were released from class about ten minutes before the other students which gave us a chance to eat before the bell rang releasing the rest of the students for their lunch period. We then stacked the trays and plates and took them to the kitchen where they got washed by some older students. The dishwashers were older, stronger kids because they used such huge, heavy pots to cook spaghetti or whatever the main dish was. After we finished cleaning the tables we were released from our duties and enjoyed the rest of the lunch break.

For that one year, District #49 would now only go to the sixth grade and closed its doors the following year, as well as all of the country schools. All of the students were transferred to Charles A. Lindberg School in Little Falls. George never attended the country school and entered first grade in town. Because they were closing all the country schools, the school system now provided bus service, which was not available for Dwaine and me. Our driveway was so long, there was no clear view or way of knowing when the bus was coming because it came from Randall. Our dad put an old car—a 1938 Chevrolet—at the end of the driveway for us to wait in because the weather could be so bitterly cold. If the bus was running late, it could be a very long time to be standing out there. The car didn't ward off any cold but did serve as a wind break. It was quite a treat to get on the warm bus after standing in the cold.

School Bus

Our dogs Shep and Rover are running to greet the school bus.
Notice how high the snow banks are.
You can see the car sitting in the field that served as our shelter.
Other side of bus, where the trees are, is where the cow pasture begins. It was a pretty long hike taking the cows out and bringing them in.

Dwaine's first day of school
In the trees beside clothesline was the outhouse.

Bette 6 and Dwaine 8
Bette's first day.

Dianne's first day: Bette 8, Dianne 6, and Dwaine 10

Mom made Bette's red cape and hat.

Judy 6, Dianne 7, Bette 9, and Dwaine 11

Judy's first day of school.

Russell's 2nd grade: Russell 7, Judy 9, and Dianne 10
The last year for District #49.

Bette 12 and Dwaine 14 started in Little Falls
High School 7th and 9th grades.

**Dwaine 15, Bette 13, Dianne 11, Judy 10, Russell 8, George 6
beginning first grade**

*All will go to Little Falls on the bus.
Bette made her skirt the year before in 7th grade.*

George and Russell

*Hey guys—nice pants, they should
last you the year. Maybe next year
too.*

Judy 5th, Dianne 6th, and Bette 8th

Another of Judy's first day

Standing in front of grain shed and collapsed building.

❧ *Chapter Five* ❧

Just Being Kids

Judy, Russell and George joined the family after moving onto the farm. Judy was born seven months later. Her St. Gabriel's hospital bill reads as follows. Notice the cost of the birth certificate:

5 days board and attendance

In Sickness at $3.00/day	$15.00
Supplies for delivery	$5.00
Medicine and Lotion	$1.30
Surgical Dressings	$2.50
Care of Babe	$2.25
Birth Certificate	$.25
Total	$26.30

Mom with baby Judy

As the weather warmed up, off would go our shoes and we preferred to never put them on again unless we went to church or back to school. We would lie in the tall grass which we pulled together and tied, using a piece of long grass as twine and it worked great, making our own tents and privacy. Nobody could find you unless you wanted to be found. We were so close to nature as we watched the bugs crawl by and the cloud formations in the sky and say "that looks like a..." on a lazy, dreamy day. Nights were warm and humid, full of the sounds of crickets and frogs croaking throughout the night. We were totally carefree and ran wild. Some may have called us a bunch of little scaredy-cat, jack-pine savages. We were pretty rough and tumble.

We could go into the woods where there was an unusual type of berry bush that grew close to the ground. The berries tasted just like wintergreen mints. We also had a choice of wild strawberries, blueberries, raspberries, chokecherries, pinch cherries, and many others. Chokecherries coated your throat if you ate too many and we always did, thus the name, they almost made you feel like you could choke. What we didn't eat, Mom made into jam or syrup and we always brought home plenty for her. In the winter we could enjoy breaking off an icicle from the maple trees and sucking on that, getting the maple flavor.

Every field and each wooded area offered its own individual form of play. One day we went in the woods with saws and hammers and started cutting sapling trees so we could build our own log cabin. It was pretty slow going until Dwaine got relieved from work and helped us. We got the four walls up but no roof which was alright because the tree branches overhead served as a roof. One of the times, we picked giant mushrooms of pretty colors and placed them along our pathway, which served as our flowers. A few days later when we went back, the mushrooms had rotted and our walls had pretty much fallen down. We didn't even try to rebuild, we just went on to another project.

We never played in the wheat fields because we would have flattened the wheat to the ground. We could play in the tall corn fields though. Corn was planted in rows, each stalk about twenty-four inches apart. You could look one way and see a straight row and you could look another way and see a straight row. Even though it seems simple, it is very easy to get turned around and not be able to find your way out. We always enjoyed playing Hide and Seek in there after it got dark, which was a game we also did in the yard because there was a multitude of places to hide.

Night time in the summer brought out the fireflies by the hundreds. They were a flying insect that lit up as they flew with their own little built in lanterns. We would catch them and rub them on our clothing where the small fluorescent lights remained and glowed. We also would put the whole bug in Mom's canning jars where they continued to flash their lights. Then we'd take them upstairs and pretend the fluorescent green lights were flashlights as they blinked on and off.

We liked to sit upstairs and pass time reading comic books. Dwaine always managed to trade and swap these books and always ended up with more than what he started with. He had a couple of big piles in his bedroom. Although we read them over repeatedly, each time was just as enjoyable as the first time. We literally wore them out to tattered paper.

We also took the Sears Roebuck and Montgomery Wards—we called it Monkey Wards—catalogs upstairs and made our own paper dolls by cutting out the dresses and putting them on another picture. Our paste was flour and water, so it was a real treat when we got real paste. It tasted pretty good too.

There weren't any screens on the upstairs windows. At night with the window open, a bat would sometimes fly in and we were scared to death of them because we'd heard so many stories about them. We'd scream and make all kinds of ruckus, chasing it with whatever we had in our hands, never daring to let them get close to us. They'd fly into one wall and then another trying to get away. The bats were always gone by the time we went to sleep. We didn't dare go to sleep with them in the house because we heard some old wives tales so often that bats will get entangled in our hair while we slept and we wouldn't be able to get them out, and also that they would likely build a nest in our hair. We would never take a chance with that.

Dwaine got a special delight in scaring us. At night, while we were upstairs in our separate bedrooms, he could talk to us easily because there were no solid walls up between the rooms. He always told the monster stories because that always put a fear in us as he weaved how the monster was going to get us. He also let us know that he had the inside scoop that we were going to be attacked by the Japanese. This was during World War II, so it sounded very possible. He was always with our dad when visitors came and he spent time with older people and listened to their conversations so we didn't doubt what he said. We lived just a few miles from Camp Ripley, the largest National Guard Training Base in the United States, so we always heard low flying airplanes over the house and farm, which just added fuel to his predictions. We went through the same ritual every night, scared to go to sleep and scared to stay awake.

The one commodity that was always in the kitchen cupboard was boxes of Jell-O. We all liked Jell-O whether made up with fruit and whipped cream or right out of the box. We'd grab a box then run upstairs with it. We always ate part of the box, but didn't eat it all because the plan was to go back later and get another mouthful. Mom would notice that the box was missing and always say the same thing in the sweetest voice. "I'll know who took the box of Jell-O because there was rat poison in it." There was no way that we were going to finish off that box, not if it had rat poison in it. So, we'd get a new box. The whole episode was repeated so many times and we had Jell-O boxes stacked up only because we didn't dare eat them.

We always had to taste everything that looked like food. We learned early in life that anything with a symbol of a skull and crossbones on it was poison and we were not to eat or touch it. Mom got some Caster Beans that she was going to plant. The only purpose for the beans was that they made a beautiful large green plant. Dianne and I found them and had to taste them. They were in a brown paper bag and there was no skull and crossbones showing that they were poisonous. We probably just bit off an end but it was enough to make us deathly sick and hallucinate. It's unlikely that we ate as much as a whole bean because eating that much could have killed us, as they are very poisonous. For years we both got ill when we saw anything made of leopard skin and we never knew why leopard skin should make us so nauseous. Those beans have a leopard skin pattern on them and I have since learned that getting nauseous when seeing leopard skin is a typical reaction.

Bette and Dianne below silo

It seems we spent our whole life running or climbing. We had a silo, which held a corn feed for the cows, called silage. The silo was just about as tall as the barn. It had a ladder that began several feet up off the ground. It was designed that way as a safety precaution to keep children from climbing it. The silo had rebar going around it, which gave a foothold to climb up to the ladder itself. After we reached the ladder and climbed up to the top, there is a landing or platform that one had to get around before continuing to the dome. The landing extended out from the side of the silo and with some careful maneuvering, I made it onto the platform and found that the view was spectacular. It was when I started back down and over the landing that I learned my first fear of height. That's when I realized that my legs weren't long enough to reach the ladder. After a long struggle, I finally was able to get myself back on the ladder but I was shaking so hard coming back down, I was sure my hands weren't going to hold me. I never climbed it again.

Russell climbed to the top of the dome, which was higher than my nerve took me. He found the same problem coming down when trying to reach the ladder with the landing in the way. He said that he started crying and our dad had to climb up and get him down. He says that Daddy, who always wore overalls, put him on his back and had him put his feet in his back pockets and wrapped his arms around his neck and how scared he was because the only thing between him and the ground was air and his feet in two pockets.

George remembers when he climbed the silo, he got to that landing and could not do anymore, including getting himself down. Dwaine had to climb up and bring him down. Dwaine says that he put George between him and the ladder and they went down one step at a time

George sleeping in the wagon that we took to the blueberry patch

This car was used as our windbreak when waiting for school bus after it wore out and stopped running.

One day we went to the far end of the cow pasture because we knew there was a large blueberry patch and we wanted some homemade blueberry pie. We took the wagon so we could bring home a big load of berries and hauled George because he could barely walk. There were five of us with visions of blueberries; Dianne, Judy, Russell, George and myself.

While the girls were busy picking berries, Russell—who could never resist teasing a bull—started to tease the bull that belonged to the neighbor. We knew from past experience that he was a very mean bull. We told him to quit, but he got such sport out of trying to get a rise out of the bull but we knew that there was nothing to worry about because the bull was on the other side of the fence.

We were still busy picking when we noticed that the bull was no longer on his side of the fence but he was on ours. He was mad, his head lowered and pawing the ground. That meant he was ready for a fight with a bunch of little kids. Everybody started running like crazy. I grabbed George by his hand and it was every man for himself. I don't think Georgie's feet touched the ground the whole distance. Dianne tried climbing trees, but never could pick the right one, either it wasn't big enough to hold her or the branches kept breaking. We finally made it home safely but our dad had to go back for the wagon and berries that we left behind, and we did get our blueberry pies although much later in the day.

Our dad put a ring with a chain attached to it in our bull's nose. The ring was permanent, but the chain was removed when he was penned up in the barn or in the cow pen. The chain prevented him from running fast or far. He had to hold his head up otherwise he stepped on the chain. The bulls were dehorned, meaning their horns were cut off so in the event that they were to catch up with any of us, they would not be able to gore us. Other farmers weren't so careful. As a safety precaution the cows were dehorned also.

We've all had our share of being chased by a bull. Sometimes it was our own bull but most of the time it was the neighbors. As soon as the bull would see us, they would start pawing the ground. Not sure if they just didn't like kids or they didn't want us to take their new found lady friends away. One time a bull chased Dwaine and he ran through the corn field zigzagging through the corn stalks.

Russell always got a special delight in teasing the bulls. This can be foolish because bulls are so mean and have a very short fuse. One day he and George were in the field at the end of the orchard and they were teasing an especially mean bull, which was rented to us for breeding purposes. Russell crawled under the barbed wire fence and into the field where the bull was grazing. He was a kind of a gangling kid, long, lean and slim. Jumping up and down and doing his antics, he knew exactly how far away safety of the fence was. The bull almost always gives a warning by lowering its head and pawing at the dirt. After a short time of teasing, the bull would charge and Russell would run as fast as he could and dive under the barbed wire. He did this several times, but one day as the bull started charging, Russell was running to the fence when his feet slipped out from under him in the wet grass and he fell to the ground. He scrambled as fast as he could on all fours to get to the fence and could feel the bull's breath on him as he made it to safety with a fraction of a second to spare. That was a pretty close call so he decided to give it up for the day. George usually stayed on the safe side of the fence and watched.

The job of getting the cows fell on the girls most of the time with at least two of us going to the pasture. The cow pasture was about a hundred acres, so it was a very large area. When we first entered through the gate, on the left (or to the west) there was a fence; and on the other side of the fence was our planted field. But going further north, that field ended and the pasture itself extended further west and met with the neighbors land, and they always had a mean bull. To the north was another neighbors' land and he too had a mean bull, this was the same bull with the blueberry picking incident. A fence with three rows of barbed wire separated all the properties. The area to the north and east was thick with brush where the cows made paths—but more like tunnels—as they made their way to the river that was also their source of drinking water.

Our dad put a couple of large salt blocks, which sat on a post off of the ground, in the cow pasture for the cows; this was done for their nourishment and to keep them healthy. When walking through the pasture it was hard to resist licking on them ourselves. Unlike the other farms, our cows were clean and they were our friends, they each had a name. But even so, we made sure that before we licked on the salt that we cleaned it first. We rarely carried any water with us, so we would spit on the salt and wipe it clean with our skirt or our sleeve and considered it good and clean.

When going to the cow pasture to bring the cows home, we'd open the gate, our minds off somewhere else when we'd notice there was a difference in the way the cows were acting. Sure enough, a strange bull got over the fence. At that point, we didn't have time to shut the gate because it wasn't a solid gate, it stretched across the opening and it was much like a regular barb wire fence having a couple of posts holding it together, loose and floppy. The bull would have had us before we got it closed and latched, or at least we were certain of that. So we'd take off running with the gate down. Sometimes we noticed a difference in the cows before we opened the gate, so we'd climb a tree and look them over; then we'd see the bull and then we'd run home but at a much slower pace because the bull and cows were safely behind the gate.

When the cows were at the gate area, it was a pretty simple job but sometimes they were deep in the pasture. One cow always wore a bell around her neck so we would listen for the sound to know which direction they were and go round them up because they always stayed together as a group. Sometimes the cow wearing the bell may be lying on the ground chewing her cud, a process in which cows regurgitate and thoroughly digest their food, and there would be no sound coming from her and it could take a long time to find them. We had to venture further into the pasture to get an idea if we should go to the west, north, or east. When the cows saw us, they would usually start heading for the gate on their own. The dog always went with us and any younger strays, he would help round them up or most often they would follow the rest of the herd. The dog was usually no help when it came to saving us from the bull—or at least we didn't stick around long enough to find out.

The cows attracted a lot of mosquitoes. When we'd start walking home, the mosquitoes would swarm around our heads. Above each head was a big dark cloud consisting of hundreds of them. They didn't set on us or bite as long as we kept moving but made their attack as soon as we stopped. It was a good incentive to keep moving as fast as we could. The cows were always anxious to get back home and into the cow pen and barn because they looked forward to getting milked.

Russell remembers how he and George would play in the pigpen. Russell would stand on the wooden fence between the cow pen and the pigpen. He would then have George chase the pigs toward him and as they passed by, he would jump off the fence onto their back wrapping his arms around their necks and getting a pretty good ride until the pig shook him off, which made it time to try it with another. These kinds of things were done while our dad was in the fields or out of sight because he would never have allowed them to do this. Not for the pigs safety, they were large strong animals but for ours.

When our dad worked in the fields, he always stirred up some animal nests. Sometimes the animals were injured from the farm machinery. When this happened we would take the animals to our Mom and she would tear some strips of fabric and doctor them. Most of the time they were gone by morning and we figured they got away again as usual. Most likely what happened was they didn't survive the night and she disposed of them, or she didn't want them to survive and she disposed of them. Then she wouldn't have to listen to the wailing and crying while we performed a funeral for our new friend. Although we never attended a funeral, we knew that it was necessary to go through this ritual. Field mice were in large supply. Although Mom didn't appreciate them, they were better than regular house mice because they had a shorter nose making them a lot cuter. They usually disappeared too, but maybe not on their own.

Every summer, we had the cutest baby rabbits. They usually lived long enough to run away when they got the chance. One time we decided that a baby rabbit we caught was not going to run away so we put it in the basement. With the dirt floor, it did get away and we were never able to catch it again. He was still living down there when we moved away. There was plenty of food for him with all the potatoes, carrots and rutabagas, if they even eat rutabagas.

Dianne, Judy, and I were in the barn and came across a mother cat giving birth to her third kitten. The first two were already in her nest. We'd watched the veterinarian give aid to the animals so we made the decision that she couldn't possibly do this without our help. I guess we scared her when we grabbed hold of the unborn kitten because she moved out of the nest. We were just going to pick her up and put back in her nest but she started to run. So we ran after her. She ran all the way from the barn to the chicken house where she crawled underneath and we couldn't reach her. Well, if we couldn't help her, we'd take care of those two babies. We gathered them up, took them to the house and tried to give them milk; after all, they had to eat something. Our little patients were in trouble and it soon became obvious that they weren't going to live. We gathered around them, crying and praying so hard, but our prayers were unanswered. They received the nicest funeral with their own little cardboard box caskets filled with flowers. The mother cat survived the ordeal we put her through, but the last kitten didn't.

Bette with Robby the bird on her knee

We were in the pine tree section near the barn when we spotted a robin's nest and it was fairly low to the ground, at least within climbing reach. All we wanted to do was to look in the nest and see the babies as we climbed the tree. We found three of them in there. Two of them got away but we brought one home with us and named him Robby. Before he was fed, we'd call him by that name, and then he'd chirrup and open his mouth. We caught lots and lots of worms for him before he was able to fly off by himself and then he could catch his own. For the rest of the summer, we would call him by his name while holding his worm, and he'd fly down to get it. He came back to the same tree in the yard every year and answered our call but never came near us again not even for a tasty worm.

One day Mom came into the chicken house and caught Dianne, Judy and I just laughing and having a good time. We were breaking eggs and feeding them to the chickens. Once a chicken gets the taste of their egg, they'll break the egg themselves and eat them. When it's an occasional chicken, our dad would make up an egg for them and add pepper to it, which cured them right away from breaking any more. In this case, we had a few hundred chickens that were going to develop a very bad habit. The only thing he could do was to catch each chicken, then cut the tip off the upper beak, blunting the end. The bottom part of the beak was left intact, which wasn't as hard in substance as the top and they were unable to break an egg. Daddy, Mom and Dwaine worked through the night catching and trimming every beak. The main income we had in the winter was from the sale of the eggs, so when we did that foolish act, we really jeopardized our livelihood.

Dianne remembers when she got to stay in the house and wash dishes, so Judy and I were sent to the chicken house to feed the chickens and gather the eggs. It seems that we weren't real happy with that arrangement and the next time Dianne went to the chicken house, she saw that someone had taken a green crayon and drew a picture of a pig on the wall. According to her it even had a curly tail. Written beside it was 'Dianne is a pig'. She says it hurt her little feelings. I know Judy and I felt better though.

It seems that we always had to try something new even if it was not real smart. Dianne and I were washing eggs and she wondered if one would fit in her mouth and so she put an egg in her mouth. This was a whole egg with the shell on it and it slipped in and over her teeth so easy. Getting it out was a different matter as the two of us kept trying to get it out but we just couldn't get it back over her teeth. The only way we did get it out was by breaking it while it was still in her mouth and then she was spitting raw egg and shells. That was never tried a second time.

Dianne and I were walking around the yard barefoot and I felt the familiar squish between my toes of stepping in fresh chicken poop. That was one of the hazards of walking barefoot and just reason enough to make you run to get a pair of shoes. We sat down on the grass so I could pull wet grass, which was always handy and worked well for cleaning up. I saw a great opportunity and thought I was being funny, at least I was laughing, and I shoved my toe in her mouth expecting to get a gagging and spitting from her. But I didn't laugh for long because she clamped her teeth down on my big toe just like a snapping turtle and I was beginning to feel very lucky to get out of that predicament in one piece. She did a royal job of turning the tables on me and I was the only one squealing.

On Sunday's Mom usually cooked a big meal, always being ready for unexpected guests. We didn't have a telephone and visitors could pop in at any time without notice. Some visited for a while and others joined us with a meal. Farm work was set aside for the day. One day when cousin Joanne was visiting, it must not have been Sunday, but we decided that we wanted a chicken dinner and Mom would cook it for us. So we caught the chicken but then we had to chop its head off and clean it before bringing it to her. So we laid it across the chopping block and with Joanne holding the chicken, I swung the ax. Oops, missed, tried again. Ax turned sideways and only caused injury. Every time I would bring the ax down, the chicken would move trying to get away. We weren't having much luck until Dwaine came along and did it for us along with another one and Mom cooked us our chicken.

The only wild meat we ate was deer known as venison and grey squirrels but we also shot wild pheasants, ducks and geese. I enjoyed going hunting in the woods with Dwaine for squirrels, which was always in winter with the trees bare of their leaves so it was easy to spot them in a tree. Sometimes Dwaine had to climb the tree to retrieve the squirrel that got hung up on one of the branches as it was falling to the ground. Mom could skin and gut a squirrel in the blink of an eye. We would get enough to fill a roasting pan and she would cook them, making a very good meal. Dwaine had visions of getting rich one day by selling the furs. He'd use the tails for ornaments mounted on his cap or his bicycle.

Our dad was in his deer stand during hunting season when he spotted a deer and shot it. Sometimes it may take a while to find where the deer had fallen and when he found it, he also found that a wolf beat him to it and the wolf was laying claim and it was not about to give it up. It was a very large aggressive wolf taking a stand to keep its prize, so our dad shot it too. We could sometimes hear them howling in the wintertime but we never saw any.

Our dad shot this deer and wolf in our woods

The wolf is almost as big as the deer.

We received word that our Aunt Jessie was sending us a package in the mail and we were so excited about getting it. We believed she had a more than a comfortable living condition in Texas, so we could only imagine the presents that would be coming our way and we couldn't wait to get

it. Nobody went to the mailbox that day, which was close to a mile away. Dwaine and I were so sure that the box was up there and somebody would take it if we didn't go up there and bring it home.

Dwaine was twelve and I was ten when we set out in the middle of winter with a full moon. It was a cold, very cold, crisp, star studded night. Conditions were right where we could see the amazing display of Northern Lights shimmering to the north of us, when we headed down the freshly plowed driveway to get the package.

The walk wasn't too bad going to the mailbox, even though we walked past the woods that had to be full of wolves and it was the same woods that our dad shot one two years earlier. We reached the mailbox only to find that there wasn't a box or even any mail. Heading home we again had to pass the woods. Walking to the mailbox, Dwaine was so nice but now he started telling me scary wolf stories. It's possible our voices scared something because all of a sudden we could hear loud noises coming from the woods of branches breaking and something was crashing through the brush. Something very big was in there. Maybe it was a deer. But maybe it wasn't. Maybe it was a wolf.

Now Dwaine's hair is standing on end or it would have been if he wasn't wearing a cap and he is really scared. I was already scared but now I'm mind-numbing petrified. We have no protection, not even a stick or a rock and no means of finding something because everything is covered with snow. We both wanted to get home as fast as we could. We could stay on the plowed road, which made for easy walking and running if necessary, or we could try for a shortcut through the field. We decided on the shorter distance, anything to get home sooner. The shortcut wasn't faster, we found ourselves making our way through deep snow as high as our behinds. Dwaine was moving as fast as he could, but not fast enough for me.

I was dripping with fear as I was watching the trail behind me, expecting at any moment to see a wolf running up the new path we just made, and I was well aware of that fact that I'm nothing more than a piece of wolf bait at the end of the line, hoping the wolf could see that Dwaine was bigger than me and had more meat on him. It became too late to turn around and go back to the road and it would also have put us nearer to the woods where we heard the noises, so we had no choice but to continue ahead. We finally made it into the house; empty handed, very cold, but so very thankful to be alive. A couple of weeks later the box came. It was such a big box that we couldn't have carried it. All those presents we visualized didn't exist; it was full of old clothes.

In the springtime of the year, after the snow melted and the weather warmed up, there was mud everywhere. That's because the frozen ground was thawing from down deep, and could be as much as six feet. Behind the barn was the cow pen where the cows were kept after the evening milking. This made it convenient to round them up for the morning milking. When the ground was thawing, it became a mud hole, but there was also the animal waste combined with it. Our two horses named Dick and Queenie were in the pen with the cows. Dick could be ornery and unpredictable. Russell was about six years old when he went out to the cow pen with some hay in his hand. He climbed on the wooden fence and tried to feed Dick. Dick reared knocking Russell off the fence and onto the ground and then Dick stepped on him. The ground was so full of sludge, when he stepped on him, he didn't hurt him but he pushed him right down into the muck and cow manure. He looked like a little walking tar baby, covered from head-to-foot with mud and manure. Dianne couldn't understand why Mom didn't just throw him away rather than try to clean him up because she wouldn't have touched him.

Whenever the car started or a wagon moved, we thought we had to be in it even if it were for a short distance. This was what happened when Judy climbed into the car, but she didn't shut the door securely. Our dad was only going to back the car up the hill. Because the ground was so muddy, he had to gun the engine so he wouldn't get stuck. When he backed up, the door flew open and Judy fell out of the car. The front wheel ran over both her legs but because the ground was so muddy, she sunk right into the ground and had no injuries.

We lived about ten miles from Camp Ripley so we could watch the airplanes as they did their maneuvers, practices and parachute jumps. The B-17 Bombers would fly so low over our farm that we could actually see the faces of the pilots as they smiled and waved at us. We were on the ground jumping up and down, waving at them. The smaller planes, P-51 Mustang WWII fighters that dominated the wartime skies of Europe would tip their wings at us letting us know that they saw us. Often times, the smaller plane's engine would cut out and we just knew they were going to crash and it was going to be in one of our fields. We'd go running as fast as we could, excited because there was going to be a downed plane. Always before it hit the ground the engines would rev again and off they'd fly. We were so disappointed when they didn't crash.

We were all playing in the pine trees when Russell started climbing the tree with a dish towel in his hand. He was going to parachute down just as we'd watched the trainees from Camp Ripley parachuting from their planes. We watched him as he made his way to the top of the tree, but George got scared for him and tattled. Mom came out and when she saw what was going to happen she just about had a heart attack. He was about seven years old then and she talked him down. These pine trees were very tall and they had wonderful long, large branches on them. There was a time when we were all on one branch, making it go up and down and having great fun doing that until the branch broke and we all went tumbling down becoming a mass of entangled kids. Nobody got hurt except for maybe a scratch or two.

Bette, Judy, Russell, and Dianne

Admiring Dwaine's new bicycle.
Grandpa Hankes and Daddy taking it out of the box.

130

It was an exciting day. Dwaine got a beautiful, shiny, new bicycle and we were all excited for him. It would have come from Sears & Roebuck or Montgomery Wards. We purchased all our small and major products from the two catalogs. It looked like something that would be fun to ride but I was quite a bit smaller than he was and it was a boy's bike. I finally got the nerve one day to try to ride it. I was heading down the driveway but my legs weren't quite long enough to do a full circle with the pedals or use the brakes. I had a hard time trying to keep it going forward and I couldn't stop it. When I realized that I may never get off this dangerous vehicle I headed it for the ditch for a softer crash landing. I decided that I would leave his silly bike alone for a long time as I limped home.

We were fascinated with anything that was bright and shiny and our fingers itched to touch it. Of special interest were the pretty assorted colored lightening rod bulbs that were located at the top of the house. We never could get close enough to reach them. Toys were few and far between, we just didn't have many so we devised our own. The jar lids became our dishes while playing house. An oatmeal box became an excellent quiver holder for our arrows, which was a straight stick found in the woods. A flexible branch and a piece of string became our bow. A fork in a tree branch with two strips of inner tube rubber was our slingshot. We created our own slide by sliding off the tin roof of the pig barn and dropping off onto the ground below which was always soft dirt that the pigs kept turned over and hopefully we wouldn't land on one of them. It was only by luck that we didn't get cut from any jagged pieces of tin.

Our Uncle Orlo Hankes was still single and in the Army when he visited with us. He brought us a sleek, pretty, metal car that we operated with pedals. Very nice. Only toy we ever had that we weren't able to take apart. He was playing with me and although he was never mean, for some reason I started to cry. Dianne never liked anyone picking on her sisters or brothers, so she picked up a piece of coal and threw it at him hitting him in the forehead. She told him "You're never going to go to Heaven and be an angel." He brought that up to her for the rest of his life and always chuckled about it. She was pretty good at wielding the pieces of coal because once I was swinging on a rope and wouldn't give it to her so she threw a piece of coal at me and hit me in the forehead splitting it open.

Judy took a nasty fall when she was swinging as high as she could go with the rope in the front yard. She remembers that she saw lots of stars. Judy also had a unique ability. She could climb a rope by putting the rope between her toes and climb right up, no matter how high. Daddy was always so tickled when he would watch her do that and whenever he had company over, he always wanted Judy to show them—and they were always pretty amazed.

If our parents were going to be gone for some time, they got a sitter to stay with us, but the sitters lived a distance away. Most of the time, they would have errands to do in town and left us home alone. Dwaine was a real good brother and other times he was a really bad brother. They wouldn't be halfway down the driveway and the torture would begin. He'd throw blankets over our heads, trying to suffocate us. Twist our arms and any other limb he could. Push us down the steps into the spooky basement with the monster and then latch the door so we couldn't get out.

What a relief it was when we saw the dust cloud from a car coming down the road. He knew our parents were returning and nobody would ever believe how really nice he would become. He always offered us a nickel or half a candy bar if we wouldn't tell; rarely would it be a whole candy bar. He owes us a truck load of half candy bars and an awful lot of nickels because he never paid up and we never told on him. Our dad's treatment could be harsh with Dwaine and we never wanted to see him in any trouble. As a young boy Dwaine was able to do most any job that a man could do. Therefore more was expected from him, perhaps unfairly, and when he fell short, it wasn't taken into account that he wasn't a man, but he was still just a young boy.

Every year Little Falls hosted a county fair where we as students entered our art pieces and Dwaine was a member of Future Farmers of America entering his pigs, bringing home the blue ribbons. When Dwaine was in the 9th grade, he sold candies and soda pop for the FFA, walking around the fair, hawking their goods, and he had the highest sales so as a reward he came home with a new FFA jacket.

One year we went to the State Fair in Minneapolis. Our dad drove to the Nelson's to ask Monnie and Ethel if Dale could join us. Monnie would have replied in his thick Swedish accent that sounds like music to the ears, "Yah, I tink dat vould be fine". Dale was so excited about going he couldn't go to sleep and he couldn't go to sleep because he was afraid he wouldn't wake up at 4:00 in the morning when we would be heading out. We arrived at the fair very early before they were open, and parked at the gate entrance.

Beside Dwaine getting a new saddle for less than $10, two things stand out in our memories. One of the attractions was a woman that had two heads or four legs or something very different about her, most likely she was a Siamese twin. We wanted to see her but it cost a quarter to get in and we didn't have enough money. It was decided that Dianne and I would pool our money with Dwaine so he could go in and then tell us what he saw when he came out.

There was no cure for polio, which is a highly infectious disease caused by a virus. It invades the nervous system and can cause total paralysis in a matter of hours. Polio infections lead to irreversible paralysis, usually in the legs and the breathing muscles become immobilized. For the first time we saw a young woman living in an iron lung, a tank respirator which did the breathing for her. Her whole body was in a cylindrical chamber except for her head.

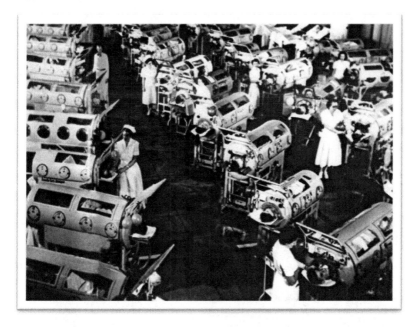

Patients in iron lung machines in a hospital ward

Invention of machine about 1930.

Mom had just passed her twenty-fourth birthday when Georgie was born. She was now the mother of six and the oldest wouldn't turn nine for another five months. What a handful. Grandma Pierzina stayed with us while she was in the hospital for the birth of our little brother. When he was brought home from the hospital, it was so thrilling. It was a little baby just like one of my dolls but so much better. I was six years old and I asked Mom if I could have him. She let me believe that he was my very own baby and I just loved him so much. I thought I did everything for him but as the years go by, I know that I couldn't possibly have. George remembers when I was giving him a horsy-back ride, then he wanted down but I didn't want to put him down. He got angry with me so I more or less dumped him off, right onto a piece of glass and split his knee wide open. Looks like my motherly love ran a little thin. He had to be pretty big because he remembers the incident and the cut on the knee from the piece of glass, but then again it was a very deep cut.

Bette with her real live doll—Georgie Porgie

There were a couple of times when our parents hunted for lost kids. The first one was Dianne. They were in the sheep pasture picking berries when they realized that Dianne wasn't around anywhere. It was a low lying area of soft waterlogged ground. Every so often there were clumps of firmer soil and grass. Finally they found the two-year-old curled up on a clump of grass. She was sound asleep. Mom remembers how scared she was.

The second time was my fault and was I in trouble. The whole family was out picking berries and they didn't want George out there where they couldn't keep an eye on him, so I had to stay by the car and babysit for him. He was pretty little, maybe two years old. We were not on our property, so it was unfamiliar grounds. I remember watching an insect called a Walking Stick in the branch of a tree. They were a large bug that looked like a stick and I was fascinated by them because I had never seen anything like that before. Next thing I knew, my parents came back to the car and George was gone with no clue as to which way he went.

We looked for him for a long time and finally found him in the woods. I never thought of George as a little brat ever, but for the first time I thought he was and could have stayed in the car.

When the guys were working on 'The Sixty-five,' the additional land that was purchased later, it was quite a distance to drive home with the horses or the tractor for the noon meal because they moved so slow and good working hours would have been wasted. Mom would pack a lunch, fill the car with kids and we would drive out to them. We'd spread a blanket under the trees and have a little time to spend with our dad and brother.

We always enjoyed when Mom would pack a basket of sandwiches and we would go by the river bank and have a picnic lunch. The Little Elk River ran through our cow pasture and I'm not sure if we were on our land or just next to it. The spot was at the bend in the road when going to our house so the farm wasn't out of sight and not far away but we did drive the car there. Mom never learned how to swim and our dad could swim somewhat and none of us kids learned. Our dad would take a bar of soap and get in the water and wash up. He would check out the river bed for any low spots and then we could join him. It was always a treat to get away and the setting was so pretty.

Russell and George often walked through the fields with our dog Shep. One day they made it to the river. While they were playing along the bank, George fell in. Shep jumped into the water and pulled him out. The fastest way we could get a spanking was to disobey and going to the river was disobeying big time. Our dad would leave whatever he was doing, whether he was in the field working the crops or doing a project around the farm, he would stop whatever it was and come to us and give us a spanking. Dianne, Russell, and George found that out the hard way when he spotted them heading down the road toward the river. With six kids running around it was a little hard to keep watch on everything we did, but he did keep a watchful eye.

A girl named Audrey and I became friends after I entered school in town. She was a city girl and never experienced farm life, so she came home with me to spend the weekend. Audrey, Dianne, Judy, and I were walking down the road and we came to the river and sat on the bank. Audrey told us she could swim but we admitted that we did not know how so she wanted to show us and she got in the water. It soon became apparent that she really didn't know how to swim; and at first we thought she was playing around. She was in deep water over her head and the current was carrying her away and she was struggling very hard. We held a long stick out to her which she grabbed a hold of and we pulled her back on shore. Looking back, it's obvious that Audrey was of a frail body, light as a feather; she was not a strong, robust girl. It's frightening to think that this could have had a very different ending.

Uncle Clarence, our dad's brother, would sometimes stop by our farm to see if Dwaine could be relieved from his work to help him, which Dwaine was very excited about doing. Clarence ran a bait shop out of his home that was located about a half mile from Camp Ripley and the soldiers and other patrons would come and buy minnows to use as bait when they went fishing. They caught the minnows in small streams, standing in the water using a net with poles on each side with Dwaine on one side and Clarence on the other and when they lifted the net up, it would be full of minnows or that was what they were hoping for. These minnows were then transferred into a tank on the pickup with water that was constantly circulating otherwise the minnows would have died. After getting them home they were transferred into large tanks with fresh icy water flowing twenty-four hours a day. Along with planting and selling crops, this is how Clarence earned a living. He had one cow and a few pigs; he also raised mink and worked for the Minnesota Conservation Department tagging deer.

In the cow pasture there was an area that was part of the river but it was very shallow and always held a lot of little water critters. We were able to find and catch pollywogs and minnows.

The river had another critter that we didn't like though, blood suckers, better known as leeches. When the slimy black things would attach themselves to our leg, depending on how large they were, they were sometimes hard to get off. We might have to wait until we got home to pour salt on them and they released themselves leaving a red circle on our skin.

The ditches on both sides of the driveway had water where cattails grew and there were lots of pollywogs. They soon began to develop legs and feet and their tails shrunk in size and shortly disappeared as they became a frog and we would catch them too. The ditches were better because they were closer to home and no bloodsuckers.

We had a couple of nuisances that we had to contend with along with the blood suckers and that were the horse flies which had a nasty bite that hurt for a long time and the multitude of mosquitoes. When a mosquito landed on our arm, we would watch them fill with our blood and then we'd smack them. A walk in the woods usually meant that in a short time we could feel something crawling on us and that meant that we carried home a wood tick or a few more. We would then burn them with a match because that was the only way to get rid of them. On any farm there are always a lot of flies and we had them too.

Although there were plenty of cats on the farm, they weren't pets as much as they were a necessity. Their purpose was to catch mice and rodents. Sometimes they would carry off a chicken and when they were caught, they were instantly shot. We shed a quick tear but that's the way it was. No amount of pleading could spare them; chickens were part of our livelihood.

We may not have had many pets, but we each had a cow of our own. Judy had a young bull that she named Umjay and his pen was right under the stairs that went up to the hayloft. When Umjay had a birthday, she made him a special treat of ice cream and mixed oats in it for him. This must have been after we got electricity because before that we didn't have a refrigerator or freezer and ice cream had to be eaten right away so it wasn't often that we got that treat. She was so disappointed when we moved and she couldn't take him with her.

We just loved it when our cousin Tom Pierzina would come over. We'd get him up on the stairs and then he was afraid to come down because of Umjay. We'd all be down already and tell him all the dire consequences that were going to befall him as soon as he tried it. That bull would never have hurt anyone, mostly because he was very young. My cow was named Bess and was a great milk producer, giving more milk than most. She was a gentle heifer and I could spend hours laying on her back. Most of the cows were gentle animals.

One of our favorite pastimes was to grab the tail of a frisky young cow and make them run. Dianne was doing that when she fell on a rock and broke her collarbone; she was about eight years old. The cow pen had only one rock in it and she found it. Dwaine and I were there when that happened and she asked me what she did after the fall. I told her she cried. She remembers lying under a tree not wanting to move and then she holed up in the little bedroom and wouldn't come out. We didn't tell our parents and in a couple of days, they noticed that something was really wrong. Not sure if it was because she could not use her arm or if her shoulder was hanging funny but she wouldn't admit to anything, she did not want to go to the doctor. She had a break in the bone which was visible just looking at it; the bone had a separation in it. She was taken to the doctor and had to wear a brace for several weeks.

She was quite a bit younger when Dwaine remembers that Dianne tried to milk the horse. It was not a mare. When she reached toward him, Dwaine thought the horse was going to knock her over in trying to get away from her. Dianne doesn't remember it but she knows for a certainty that Dwaine set her up on that one.

Dianne and I played together a lot when we were kids. Although there was a lot of playing, there was also a fair amount of scrapping. And boy could we tangle. She was mad at me about something and I don't know where the idea came from but I just wanted to get back at her. I looked at her seriously and told her that she didn't have any right to fight with me because she wasn't really my sister and that Mom and Daddy found her in the cow pasture. That really stopped her and I thought it was pretty neat. She wanted to know the details so I told her that they found her behind a rock so they brought her home and kept her. She was crushed. She started crying and cried for quite a while and I didn't tell her different. Mom couldn't figure out what was wrong with her and Dianne finally asked if it was true. Well it wasn't and she was so glad to hear that.

There was one time when we were visiting with Grandma and Grandpa Hankes. When walking into their house, it always smelled of Noxzema and cigars and that was a wonderful smell. Although it was afternoon, we kids with our cousins were going to play a game of Hide and Seek, a game we usually played after dark. Grandpa saw what we were doing and gave specific instructions that we were not to go in his hayloft. He didn't say why but the reason was that loose hay was covering over the holes that were cut out in the floor as a means of getting the hay down to the lower section. This is normally not a problem to the worker who knows where the holes are. I'm thinking, oh how perfect, nobody will find me there and I headed up the ladder and moving further into the loft, I felt a swoosh as my feet went out from under me and I landed on the floor below just as Grandpa was walking through with a pail of milk from milking the cow. Had he taken a couple of steps further, I would have landed on his head; instead I landed on the floor right in front of him. He scooped me up and took me outside and laid me out on the hay rack and that's where I was when I came to again.

A little tale about our grandpa. He had a well that he no longer used and wanted to take the pump out but he had to cut the 220 electric wires leading to it. He thought maybe if he could take the axe and swing it real fast and hit the wire real fast that he would be able to cut the wire in half. So he decided to try it. When he saw daylight again, he found himself slammed up against the wall of the barn.

Our hayloft offered many, many hours of fun and play. This hayloft had nice flooring, real nice flooring. It seems that the previous owner used the hayloft for a dance floor and put on dances with music and drinks on a regular basis. It was empty of hay by the spring time of the year and was a vast open area. Later it became filled with hay and that was as much fun as it was when it was empty because we could roll down hills of hay or just get a blanket and lay in the hay and talk. And you could smell the wonderful fresh cutting of the hay.

On the top of the barn was a steeple with a weather vane on top of that. One day we were in the empty hay loft and George asked Russell to go up in the steeple and bring him back a bird's nest that was up there. It was a very long way up to the top of the ceiling. Russell climbed up the side of the wall and grabbed onto the rail that ran the length of the barn. With hand over hand and his feet also on the rail, he shimmied himself across to the steeple to get Georgie his prize. It's a wonder he didn't fall, and a good thing because he would have landed flat on his back on the hard floor. He then had to shimmy his way back to the wall with the nest. I don't know why he didn't just grab hold of the rope and we could have pulled him over to the steeple because there was a wheel on top of the track, instead we all just watched him.

Dianne and I were playing in the empty hayloft with our dolls when we decided that it would be fun to jump out the small door onto the ground below. The thought crossed our minds whether or not we'd be injured and we were wondering about that. So we threw a doll down onto the cement pad below and it seemed to fare just fine, therefore we would too. We were going to do this together so holding hands; we were doing a countdown when Grandpa Hankes happened to come around the corner and stopped us, very likely saving us from injury. She remembers that there was some hay below but I remember seeing the rubber doll on cement.

Dianne also reminds me of the time that we were in the empty hayloft swinging from a rope. She was hanging upside-down while I was holding the other end of the rope. I was sitting on top of the oat bin which was about eight feet high off the floor, maybe to give me some leverage; there must have been a good reason. She must have lipped off at me because I let go of the rope. She came crashing down onto the hard floor on her head. She wasn't that high off the floor but a few feet would be enough to feel the bump. Doctors have questioned her about being in some sort of accident and told her that she must have been in an accident because she has issues with her spine. She thinks that maybe it's possible that perhaps the problems were caused from that fall.

My aunt's nephew, Larry was visiting her from Michigan and she thought he would enjoy spending the day with us so she brought him over and then she left. I'm not sure what long range plans were made but I don't think they turned out as they planned. The barn was full of hay and we were all playing up there. There was a lot to do, swinging from ropes and dropping in the hay was always lots of fun, and I would not have been wearing a dress doing that. Larry ruined a really fun day; he planted a kiss right on my mouth. I was still a blissfully innocent girl. I let out a screech and I was mad. Larry took off running and I went screeching after him. He got down from the hayloft and was running down the driveway and I was right behind him swinging a broom over my head and yelling all the way. I wanted nothing more than to see his head rolling in the dusty road. He outran me and I finally gave up. The only satisfaction I got was that at the end of the driveway, he turned the wrong way and he was taking a very long road to get back to his aunt's house. I'm not sure he even knew where she lived but he never came back to our house.

Our cousins, Weezie and Marie lived with Grandma Pierzina in Sobieski and always loved to come to the farm. We liked having them; they laughed a lot and were always good sports. They were a little more cautious then we were but were always game to take part. Weezie remembers when we were in the hayloft and we'd climb up the ladders and with a rope in our hands, we'd swing and go flying into a big pile of hay on the other side of the barn. She says that she only had nerve enough to swing from a short rope for a short distance.

Every summer they looked forward to school ending because they were able to spend two weeks with us. Weezie remembers that she never slept in the house, but that we only slept in the hayloft. That's probably because we didn't have any spare beds and we would have been crowded with three in a bed. Dianne and I slept in a double bed and Judy slept on a single cot. The hayloft was a much better choice. We enjoyed sleeping in a pile of hay in the barn at night, where we could talk for hours and dream of what the future may hold for us. We'd listen to the sounds around us among others, the crickets chirping, the frogs croaking and the owls with their all night vigils. We were able to tell what the temperature was by counting the cricket chirps. After a good night's sleep, and getting up the next morning we'd have hot cereal with fresh thick cream and ready for another day.

Judy, Dianne, Weezie, Bette, Russell, and George on the ground

Picture taken in our orchard.

Dianne with dad on a return visit to Gillette Hospital in St. Paul.

She looks so small next to her dad.

What a sad little face on Dianne

She did not like seeing a doctor.

Bette with Russell and George and Shep

Mom wrote:
Georgie disappeared one morning and I found him in the orchard as nude as the day he was born so I gave him a lilac branch and took his picture. The branch was a bit too big though.

Dwaine, Bette, and Dianne

After a heavy rain, our driveway overflowed, so we put on our shorts and went swimming...or so we thought.

Dianne, Dwaine, and Bette

All nice and clean after a refreshing muddy swim.

Russell with his dad on tractor

Dianne, Judy & Russell in front

Dwaine with his new bicycle

Giving his little brothers a ride

Russell and Tom Pierzina playing in sand

Later in time Tom would one day buy the house that was located on the other side of the tall tree on right. Same house we broke all the windows out.

Judy, Bette, and Joanne with little boys Russell and Tom

Russell with birthday cake

We each always got a nice big birthday cake. Maybe no presents, but always a cake.

Dianne with her birthday cake

April 3, snow on ground.

Georgie sipping a beer. Uncle George watches

Working at getting the hang of it. Russell in back

Russell, Daddy, Grandma Pierzina, Marie, Uncle George

Uncle George with Mom

Back row: Judy, Bette, Joanne, and Dianne

Front row: Russell, Tom Pierzina, Jim Hankes, Terry Pierzina, Jeannie Hankes, and George

Picture taken up on the hill, corn crib in background.

152

Judy, Weezie, Dianne, Bette (Russell and George in front)

Birthday cake for Russell

Back row: Bette, Joanne, Dianne

Front: Russell behind bush, Jeannie Hankes, Peggy Swanson in front of Terry, Judy

Front: Jimmy Hankes & George

Back row: Dianne, Joanne, Bette, Judy Middle: Russell, Jeannie, Terry Front: Jimmy, Peggy, and George

Judy, Bette, Dianne, Dwaine

Mom called them "The Three Graces"

Judy, Aunt Doodie, Dianne

Dresses were made from chicken feed sacks.

Bette

Terry and Tom Pierzina's birthday party

Back row: Bette, Joanne, Weezie, Dwaine
Middle row: Neighbor girl, Judy, Dianne, Marie
Front row: Jimmy Hankes, Terry, Tom, Russell, George.

Dianne, Bette, Judy, George, and Russell in front
Sitting on bales of straw.

Judy watching Russell ride the horse, Queenie

In background is the field of corn that we crossed to get to the sheep pasture on our way to school.

Russell, Judy, school friend - Punky Bowman, Dianne

Dianne calls this the Hillbilly picture–no shoes.

***Judy & Dianne with a couple
of geese***

Russell and Judy in 1942 Chevy, with Shep and Rover

*Rover had the misfortune of being in the field when mowing was
being done and all four legs were cut.*

*He was carried home and taken to the vet and came home all
bandaged, his injuries too severe to survive.*

Dwaine, Russell, and George

The field right behind them was the shortcut we took when trying to get home before the wolf got us. Further back, across the road is the field that Dwaine overturned the tractor and the same field that he broke the wheel on the tractor. Trees in background are the cow pasture and encompasses from the left of photo to the right of photo.

Dwaine, Bette, Dianne, Judy, Russell, and George

Judy

Dwaine, George, and Tom Pierzina

❧ Chapter Six ❧

Religion

Dwaine, Bette and Dianne were baptized in St. Stanislaus Kosta Catholic Church in Bowlus, MN. Judy and Russell were baptized in St. James in Randall and George was baptized in St. Gabriel's Hospital before he came home. He was born in February and the weather was severe and he was coming home after a storm.

All or most of the family attended Mass every Sunday at St. James. At that time Mass was only said in Latin. Our prayer book, or missal as it was called, was written in Latin. On the opposite page you could find the English version. It was a church rule that the girls and ladies always wore a hat or scarf on our heads. You could not enter the church without having your head covered. On the rare times that we forgot the hat or scarf we would bobby-pin a handkerchief on our head.

Confession was once a month as required by the church. The priest sat on one side of a thin wall in the confessional and we kneeled on the other side with a wire screen between us. He could not see us while we confessed our sins. We thought that if we confessed a lot of sins with big numbers like fifty-six times, it was a better confession so we'd get together and decide how many times we would say we did it because we didn't want to use duplicate numbers. We would admit to anything that sounded like a sin to make the list longer. We didn't know what the word adultery meant but it was one of the Ten Commandments so it was

162

a sin. I don't remember if we ever confessed to that one but I can only imagine hearing the priest choking with the admission of committing adultery forty-seven times from an eight and nine year old. One sin we could always confess was that we disobeyed our parents but we really didn't; only a fool would have disobeyed our dad. Another good sin was that we lied but that was most often saying that we had a stomach ache to get out of a chore or school. Mostly our lie was, "She hit me first". Probably the biggest sin we had was telling the priest a lie in the confessional when we told him that we lied and disobeyed so many times.

The old church rules were much stricter than they are now. We were not allowed to eat or drink anything before receiving communion. If you did either, you could not receive. The thought of going to hell was too much to disobey. The farmers had to do their chores before getting ready for church. It meant a very early morning rise and then they had to go to church without breakfast or even a cup of coffee. Another rule was we could not eat meat on Fridays.

During Mass, all the kids had to sit in the front rows, girls on one side and boys on the other with parents in the back of the church. Usually we went to an early Mass but occasionally we attended the later Mass which was called High Mass. During High Mass, the priest threw off incense which always made us sick and always made Dwaine pass out. He'd be standing or sitting and down to the floor he would go every time and had to be taken out of church. As kids, we thought that was why they put us in front so the parents wouldn't get sick.

Each family was required to pay a pew fee of $1 per week. After we sold the farm, my dad held a receipt for $150 in arrears for the past eleven years, which he then paid. There were times they only put a quarter in the collection envelope because they didn't have a dollar. A statement was passed out at the end of each year showing how much money each family paid during the year, which brought shame and embarrassment to the family that didn't live up to their part. The statement always showed that our Uncle Orlo and Aunt Betty Hankes donated $52, they were one of the few families that did and one year they were the only family.

Priests and nuns were so strict then. Father Fadruski would twist our ears if we didn't know our assignment or couldn't answer a question or repeat a prayer. I always prayed so hard that if he asked me a question that I would know the answer. One Sunday we were at Mass when there was a little girl in the pew behind us crying. We turned around to see what was wrong. The priest sent the altar boy down and told us, "Father wants to see all of you after services." There were three rows of kids and we were all pretty scared because the altar boy blocked our way from leaving after Mass was over. Father gave us heck up one side and down the other but he didn't twist our ears for which we were grateful. We told him that a little girl was crying and he told us that he didn't care what was going on behind us, that we were never to turn our faces away from the alter. Years later a couple of rules were changed. We could eat in the morning as long as it was one hour before receiving communion and we were now supposed to adjust to the new rule, giving the Sign of Peace in which you greet everybody around you, including those in the pews behind you, which meant turning our face away from the alter.

We attended Catechism every Saturday. After school let out for the summer we didn't get a break at all. We had to go to Catechism for two weeks, Monday through Friday and maintain the same hours as we did in school. The biggest difference was the walk was a lot longer and the days were hotter. We always got a ride into Randall but most of the time we walked home.

One day when I was in about the third grade, I was given a nickel to spend at lunch time. I knew exactly what I was going to spend it on. There was a store near the church and they sold something new called popsicles and I couldn't wait to get one. As soon as we were able to go outside again, I headed straight for the store and just barely got it out of its packaging when we were all called back into the church again. It wasn't lunch time; it was only recess. I didn't know what to do with my popsicle and I wanted to save it for lunch time, so I put it in my jacket pocket. In a short amount of time, it was melting and sugar water was dripping all over and I was sticky. The nun told me to go back outside and eat it but there wasn't much left because it had turned to liquid. What a disappointing turn of events for me.

We all received our First Holy Communion at St. James, except George because he was in California at seven years old. Judy was selected to be an Angel twice for the First Communions but one of the times, they didn't notify Mom, so she was not prepared and didn't have a white dress for her. The other time she was an angel was when Dianne received her First Communion.

The day I was to receive my First Holy Communion and before I got dressed, I was sent to the chicken house to feed the chickens. While I was in the feed room, without thinking, I put one wheat kernel in my mouth and ate it. Then I was horrified because we were not supposed to eat anything before receiving communion. How could I tell my mother that I cannot receive? The dress and veil were sitting there for me to put on and she put so much work into getting them ready. I would have had to wait another whole year before the next class would be ready. There was to be a big dinner celebration with lots of company. It was with such dread that I continued with the plans and put on my new dress, but my beautiful day was ruined. I was so sure God was going to strike me dead when I received the host with this black mark on my soul and I was going to spend eternity in hell. From my catechism I learned that he was a vengeful, wrathful God but in time I learned that he was a forgiving, loving God

Dwaine, Bette, and Dianne received Confirmation together. Dwaine wore a suit and Dianne and I wore yellow, dotted Swiss dresses. We had to select a Saint's name, I chose Louise, Dianne chose Elizabeth, and Dwaine chose Anthony in honor of our sponsors; Grandma Louise Pierzina, Aunt Betty (Elizabeth)

Hankes, and Tony Wenzel, a family friend and neighbor from St. James.

   Our grandmother Louise Pierzina lived in Sobieski; she was a soft-spoken, very mild person. When she spoke she almost had a purr to her voice. It was through her that we learned a love for our religion. We always wanted to go home with her and she often took us. St. Stanislaus church was about two blocks from her home and she attended Mass every single day and we attended with her and loved it. She taught us how to pray and not just say words. She taught us the beauty of the religion that we didn't get through the priests and nuns that taught us. Most important, Grandma lived her life as a religious person; her love for God and the Saints ran so deep. With her we didn't have to sit up front but we could sit with her and she explained how to follow the Latin Mass and what the meaning was behind everything they said and did. It's unfortunate that St. James felt the need to separate the children from the parents because we didn't learn the beauty of the Mass through Catechism nor under our parent's guidance because we didn't sit with them.

Dwaine's First Holy Communion

Judy, Dwaine, and Russell

Dwaine's First Holy Communion.

Bette's First Holy Communion with Mom

Bette with Daddy

Bette

Bette's First Communion classmates

Bette in back row of girls. Nuns wearing their habits–a practice that was changed years later.

Dianne's First Holy Communion

Judy served as an angel.

Judy's First Holy Communion.

George, Russell, Judy, Dianne, Bette, Dwaine
Looks like somebody didn't go to church this day.

Judy

Judy with Mom and Dad

Judy arrived at church, waiting with her First Communion classmates

Russell's First Holy Communion

Russell and Georgie

George will not receive his First Holy Communion in MN.

Russell,

(front row, far right)

Dianne, Bette, and Dwaine receive Confirmation

Judy, Marie, Bette, Grandma Pierzina, Dwaine, Weezie, Dianne

❧ *Chapter Seven* ❧

Our Home and Our Family

We were not a hugsy-kissy family. Despite that, we always felt loved and always very protected and safe even from the monster with our dad around. Mom was mild mannered while Daddy could be more volatile. He was not explosive with us kids, but Dwaine and Mom sometimes caught the brunt of his temper.

As children, we could make a lot of noise or make messes and we seldom got in trouble for it. They were lenient when it came to discipline but meant business when it was meted out, especially from our father. His greatest concern was always safety first and if we were caught doing something that we would get hurt; that most often meant a spanking to remember and remember it well. We often did many things that would have caused us injury and had we been caught, we would have carried the imprint of his hand for quite some time. Mom could be persuaded by flattery or by doing something to get her to laugh. Not so much our father but it did work sometimes, but usually with him, we had a lesson that had to be learned.

Anything we told Mom, she believed, but that's true for both parents. We could tell her we had a stomach ache when we didn't really have one but wanted to get out of some chore or school and it always worked. When she reprimanded us in public, she did it very privately; she'd talk out of the side of her mouth. Sometimes she gave us a pinch, which caught our attention but we knew that she wouldn't say or do anything while other people were around. We'd just try to stay out of her reach and not look at her, and then we could snatch that piece of candy. It wasn't long and she forgot the incident. Our dad would never, never make a scene in front of other people. We might hear about it later, though—but not Mom.

Although Mom only completed the eighth grade, she was an avid reader and became knowledgeable about so many things. She knew the answer to most any question that was asked of her. She often read to us before bedtime, choosing a book with chapters and making us anticipate the rest of the story one chapter at a time. She also read articles to us that were found in magazines such as Life magazine, which included archaeology, continents, planets, the Pyramids, and many others. We always enjoyed those interesting articles she'd find. It can be said that she was a pathfinder in new ways of thinking and instilled that in all of us.

Mom always seemed to know what we were doing, even eating the Jell-O. No matter what we were doing or getting into, she knew. She told us she had eyes in the back of her head. Dianne was always brushing Mom's hair looking for the extra pair of eyes, which she never found but was certain they were in there somewhere.

Our dad was of the belief that the most important gift you can give your children is to teach them how to work. "If they learn how to work they can accomplish anything in life and possess everything they desire, because they will always have the ability to earn it." His second bit of philosophy was, "No matter how much or how little money you make, you must put part of it in a savings account. If you don't do this, you're working for nothing." Thinking about it, he was entirely right.

Our dad would hold a coin in his hand which we could have for a kiss. He then gave us the choice of picking the coin, our choice being the nickel or a dime. He thought he could fool us, but we were too smart for him and we always picked the nickel because it was much larger than the dime. That always brought a laugh out of him and we thought he was proud of us for being so smart.

Our dad used to sing a little ditty: 'I love to go swimming with bow-legged women and swim between their legs' and Mom did not like it. He would just laugh, do a little jig and poke at her to make her laugh. We would laugh as we envisioned a pathetic, very bow-legged woman standing in the water and thinking what fun it would be to swim through them. This was a real song from the 1920's that he had in his sheet music collection from when he played the concertina as a younger man.

He always got a good laugh also when we were eating our dessert after supper, he would point to the other end of the room and say, "Look, a mouse". We would turn our head to look and he would sneak a spoonful of our dessert. We would fall for it every time and every time he would get such a chuckle.

After chores were done and he came into the house he was often greeted by a bunch of little kids who would chant, "Swing me Di". We would lie on the floor with our hands grasping our feet and he would grab a hold of the hands and feet and swing us back and forth between his legs and throw us up in the air and catch us. While this was going on with one child, there was a bunch more kids grasping their feet, chanting "Swing me Di". He never refused us by saying not now, I'm too tired, or my back hurts, although he had to be so tired and sore after a hard day's work.

Every morning we started the day with our bowl of oatmeal with fresh cream. Sometimes Mom would try to diversify and buy some Cream of Wheat or cornmeal but our dad insisted that oatmeal was the staff of life, so that was usually the cereal of choice. To make toast we put bread slices on the wood burning stove and in a short amount of time we had a piece of toast.

One can only imagine how many loaves of bread Mom baked, especially in that wood burning cook stove and so hot in the summer months. It seemed as though there always bread dough rising. She always knew just how many pieces of wood to put in the stove to get just the right temperature. There was a thermostat on the oven that showed what the temperature was but there was no dial to set so it could be a hit and miss thing, but she always seemed to get it right.

Very seldom did we have bread from the grocery store. It was such a treat for us when we got some. One day Mom must have been out of bread and didn't have any mixed, so she stopped at the store and bought a loaf while Aunt Ruby waited in the car with us. She came back to the car with the loaf of bread and was just appalled. She had to pay seventeen cents for the bread!

That wood burning cook stove served us well in a couple of other departments; it kept our young pets warm and we put our wet shoes around and under the stove. Our shoes were always wet. That stove could take a pair of fine soggy wet leather shoes and make them curl up and become hard as a rock when they dried out. Our rubbers were always wet too and bad news for the one who forgot to put either the shoes or the rubbers under the stove to dry. It's bad enough putting your feet into the hard shoes but worse if they're still wet.

Mom had little to work with but she always managed to make things bright and pretty; hanging wallpaper on the walls, making a tablecloth for the table or curtains. She was always willing to try something new, such as sewing, which she did by looking in the catalog and copying without a pattern. Feed for the chickens came in colorful cotton sacks, so we always looked forward to what the new sacks would look like. Sometimes we lucked out and there were several feed sacks of the same pattern. Then there would be plenty of fabric for larger items but generally we got a new dress. She also made doll clothes and doll blankets for us. She had a treadle sewing machine that was operated with your feet; we still didn't have electricity. One day she was sewing away and the needle went right through the center of her thumbnail. She went out to the barn where our dad was and he pulled it out with a pair of pliers. Then she went back to the house, soaked it in Lysol and returned to her sewing.

Although Mom did most of the sewing, one year she did find a lady in town who sewed for a living. She charged fifty cents for a dress and was, according to Mom an excellent seamstress. Mom bought the material and had her make up about six dresses for me when I started school. I don't remember her sewing for Dianne and Judy, so that lady may have retired or Mom was getting more experience and became a good seamstress herself.

We never went to the dentist. Toothpaste was in short supply, but we did have a toothbrush. In place of toothpaste we used baking soda mixed with salt. On the chance that we did get a tube of toothpaste, it never lasted very long with so many people using one tube. After I started school in Little Falls I went to a dentist and had some teeth filled. This dentist was located near the school and I walked to his office after school let out and Mom picked me up after she got off work, where she was employed in town. The experience was horrible because the dentist would drill the tooth and it felt like he was going to grind me all the way through the floor and through the center of the earth to China. The drilling was very loud and you could smell the smoke of burning tooth and it took forever for him to finish.

We all took a bath once a week. Water was heated on the stove and put in a metal wash tub; the same tub that was used when we washed clothes. The tub was set up on the kitchen table to make it easier for Mom to do the bathing. The littlest child, George was washed first and the same water was used for the bigger kids who followed. The water was constantly refreshed but not completely replaced so it wasn't too bad. Dwaine didn't get stuck with everybody's dirty water, there was a shower unit set up in the milk room which was used by the adults. After Dwaine and I started school in Little Falls, we took showers after gym classes.

Mom kept our hair in braids but as soon as Dianne was out of sight, she took the braids out, whether it was on the way to school or just playing. Judy and I on the other hand, walked around slanted eyed all day because the braids were so tight. I never considered taking them out because I didn't like my hair in my eyes or face. Judy's hair was very, very blond and didn't get very long but it did get long enough for braids. Dianne was blond but not as blond as Judy. My hair was down my back and auburn in color.

When we got our hair washed, Mom would do it for us. We would lay on our back on the kitchen table with our head hanging over the edge and a bucket under our head to catch the water. She would hold our head up with one hand and wash the hair with the other hand and then she would rinse our hair with vinegar water. I don't know if it's true but she believed that it would keep us from getting lice and perhaps it worked because we never did get lice but for sure we had nice shiny hair.

My hair was so thick and long that it was a pretty hard job getting it washed and rinsed, especially since we didn't have running water. One day Grandma Pierzina was visiting and we happened to be getting our hair washed at that time, and Grandma suggested to my mom, "Why don't you cut that long hair off, it would be so much easier to take care of." So she did but after the hair was cut, she was so sorry that she had.

Frequent visitors were Grandma Pierzina with Weezie and Marie. We were always excited when we saw their car coming. She was a hugsy and kissy grandmother. She never cared how dirty our faces might be. Grandma would often take one of us girls home with her for a week and we loved it. Her home always smelled of bleach, a good clean smell. Uncle Clarence and Aunt Ruby with their three children, Joanne, and twins Tom and Terry; Ruby was Mom's sister and Clarence was Daddy's brother so we were double cousins with their kids. Grandma and Grandpa Hankes came over but not as often as Grandma Pierzina and we seldom went home with them.

Everybody still remembers Mom's fried chicken dinners and what a wonderful cook she was. Not only did she make desserts for company but we usually always had dessert with our meals. In those days desserts were always included as part of the meal just as potatoes and gravy. Jell-O was always a favorite and because we had a good supply of milk we had puddings of many sorts, and always when it was our birthday, a birthday cake making our day special. We didn't always get a present, toys were not found in the stores until it was nearing Christmas, at least not in the small towns where we lived.

We all loved the fresh corn right out of the fields. We planted field corn for the animals and sweet corn for our table. While it was very young we would eat the field corn because it ripened a little sooner than sweet corn. We went to the field, picked it, cleaned it and within an hour we were eating piles of corn on the cob, dripping with fresh butter. There was always a contest to see who had the most cobs piled at the top of their plates.

Another favorite was a large frying pan full of raw potatoes and onions fried in bacon grease, most likely served with cooked rings of bologna. The potatoes were topped off with thick, fresh homemade sour cream. Bacon grease drippings were saved and used for all fried food. Maybe that's why it tasted so good. Lard was used, too, but mostly for baking.

After Mom cooked supper, she would then go outside while the rest of us ate. After a while, she would come back in the house and would tell our dad that we're having company tonight. We'd get all excited wanting to know who was going to visit us but we never got an answer. Years later we learned that this was their password, meaning that the deer were out in our fields. Then our dad would sneak out and shoot one. It was against the law to shoot out of season, so they couldn't take a chance with us kids knowing what was going on. That was most often our meat supply. The game warden was a personal friend and he could stop in at any time for a visit.

The year would have been 1944. World War II was still going strong when our parents told us that a new baby was on the way. She was pregnant with George and they were very excited. I couldn't understand that because doing a head count, they already had five. The whole country was on rations, so with a new baby, our family would get more ration stamps. You could not buy items such as sugar or gas without giving up a certain amount of stamps. They explained that even though a new baby didn't use commodities, they would be able to stretch their purchasing power. Stamps were issued according to the number of family members, not their ages. Because of the war, there were many items that people could not buy. Anything made of metal was unavailable. All metal products went to the war efforts and car production was shut down completely. Our dad didn't get drafted into the service, maybe having five kids stopped that but more important the country needed the farmers to produce the food that was needed.

It remains a mystery how our mother managed to take so many pictures. The ability to buy the film during the war years and have it developed was quite an accomplishment. Our luxuries were few and photos would be considered a luxury.

There were five sick kids with the Whooping Cough in January 1945. Mom put us all on a bed in the kitchen, and then she sat up all night in a rocking chair. She tried to read by a kerosene lantern so she could watch us and keep the fire burning in the stove. She was monstrous in her pregnancy with George and was hoping we would all be over the cough before he was born. She dreaded the thought of him getting it. We were completely recovered before his birth in February.

Another illness we had was some sort of itch. We were each bathed in the round metal wash tub in the kitchen, and then we were covered from head to foot with a dark brown medication that smelled just horrible. This medicine looked like molasses, only thicker. We went to bed in our nightwear and socks on our feet, hands, and arms. This medicine was called Will's Family

Ointment. The ingredients in it were: Petrolatum, pine tar, menthol crystals, salicylic acid, eucalyptus, and paraffin. It's no wonder we couldn't breathe. On the back of the jar is a notation to farmers: Use Family Ointment for your cow's udders. Caked or swollen and chafed teats, cuts, etc. The price on the eight ounce jar was $2.00.

Polio struck fear in the hearts of all parents then. That was before the vaccine had been found. A sore throat was one of the first signs of polio. With six of us, there were an awful lot of sore throats. Our entire family and extended family were spared this dreaded disease. Judy remembers going to the dump and there were some toys there but Daddy wouldn't let her touch them or bring them home because he was afraid that they may have been contaminated with the polio virus.

Mom was knowledgeable with home remedies and it seemed that everything healed in a short time. One of us was always stepping on a nail. It was a great relief when we felt the nail going through our shoe and stuck in the leather and not puncturing our skin. When we did step on a nail, Mom would go in the yard and get a Plantain leaf which grew wild and helped the healing process and prevented any infection. We never went to the doctor except for Dianne who saw more than her fair share and I went one time when I had a very bad case of Poison Ivy.

Easter was always an exciting time. We were sure to get something new for Easter Mass; it might be a new dress or something smaller like a hat, new socks or ribbons for our hair. We never took part in an organized Easter egg hunt and I'm not certain if they even had them but we did look for our baskets hidden somewhere in the house. Our baskets were bowls from the kitchen cupboard, always filled with three or four eggs and candy. One year one of my eggs was the most beautifully colored egg. It was far too pretty to break open so I set it on the window sill and just enjoyed looking at it. Quite some time passed, possibly even a couple of months when I decided it was time to eat it but when I cracked it open it was totally rotten inside. I didn't know hard boiled eggs would spoil.

For Halloween we never went trick or treating. The kids in town did, but we were never taken to town so we never had a chance to do that. One Halloween we decided that we would go to the neighbors and we believed that if we said trick or treat, they would have to give us candy. We never gave a thought as to whether or not they had any candy. Dwaine didn't join us but the five of us headed down the driveway to get some free candy. It was already dark when we started out and as we got to the end of the driveway we reevaluated our options. It was so cold and the walk was going to be so long we decided to turn around and go back home. It was probably a very good choice because there would be zero chances of getting any candy from a house that had six boys living in it. They would have had as much candy in their house as we had in ours, which was none.

It was nearing Christmas when Mom came home one day with a package and we were pretty sure that it was one of our presents. She hid the package and later when Mom and Daddy went somewhere, we started looking for it. We found it in the pantry, over the cupboard, and shoved way back. There were three pencil boxes and were we excited!! There was one for Dwaine, Bette, and Dianne—the three students. We each picked out the box we wanted, played with it, using the pencils, crayons, and erasures. Then we put them back and couldn't wait for Christmas. We had visions of returning to school with them and hopefully the envy of all the other kids. Mom wasn't happy when she figured out what we did and she gave those pencil boxes away to our cousins, Joanne, Tom, and Terry.

Christmas was always so exciting because Mom made it so. The anticipation was almost more than we could bear. We believed that if there was no snow on the ground, Santa couldn't come. That would mean that half the world wouldn't have a holiday, but we didn't know that. One year, it was Christmas Eve and still no snow, even after all our prayers. Mom told us that if there was no snow, not to worry because as soon as it did snow, we'd have our Christmas. It was after dark and we're each looking out the window and checking when all of a sudden it started to snow. We ran to bed so fast, totally happy and excited; we were going to have a Christmas!!

Many of our decorations were homemade, making paper chains with colored paper, stringing popcorn and cranberries. We popped popcorn by putting the corn in a wire metal container with a long handle that we'd put on top the cook stove and shake it. We'd also put two walnut shells together, then glued and painted them.

In the very early years, we never put up the tree until Christmas Eve. We didn't decorate it; Santa did that when he came. We went to bed with a bare green tree in the living room. The thrill of waking up in the morning was not only that there were presents, but there was a beautiful transformed tree too. It was truly a sight to behold, it was magical. All of our homemade ornaments and decorations were on the tree and it was completely engulfed in angel hair. Angel hair is spun glass resembling a cloud. Later years, we decorated the tree. Santa probably got the bright idea that he wouldn't have to stay up half the night at our house if it was done before he got there.

Our Christmas stockings were the biggest, longest ones we could find, usually our dad's. We didn't hang our stockings; we laid them with our name tags under the tree. We had to be certain that Santa knew whose spot was where and that we got the gifts that were due to us; because for the past week we were very, very good. Christmas morning the stockings were filled with an apple, an orange, nuts and candy. We didn't get presents in them. Usually every Christmas, the girls got dolls and the boys got trucks. Somehow Santa could always make an exact copy of what we saw in the Christmas Wish Book. We got decks of cards such as Old Maid and Authors (same as Go Fish) which we played with until they were tattered cardboard. Also Tiddly Winks, Pick-up Sticks, books, and the ever popular coloring books and crayons. There were enough goodies to keep us busy for quite a while, at least through the winter months. One Christmas morning we got up and found that the cat had diarrhea all over Dianne's pile of presents and stocking. We all chipped in and shared our candy and presents with her. The tree was never taken down until after New Year's.

For entertainment we listened to the battery-powered radio. It was turned on at the noon hour to catch the latest grain prices and local news. We also listened in the evening hours to such stories as "The Squeaking Door" and "The Shadow." Very inappropriate choices for a bunch of kids who were so scared of the monster, but we loved them. Mom listened to a soap opera called, 'The Life and Loves of Helen Trent', sponsored by Dreft soap.

In 1948 when I was ten, the presidential ballets were being counted between Truman and Dewey. The states were named, and then the count was tallied. Very long and slow process, but the most fascinating election I've ever listened to. Mom and Daddy must have voted for Truman because we were sure rooting for him. One count would put Dewey ahead and the next count put Truman ahead. I sat in front of that radio till I fell asleep sitting up and was carried to bed but I didn't want to miss a word. Truman won.

Our Dad

It was just about this same time when Mom and Daddy got ready to go out for the evening. We watched them get ready, she looked so pretty and he looked so handsome in his suit and hat and off they went. While there, Mom and Ruby with some other ladies were sitting on a bench and some guy came over and told them to give up the bench so he could use it. The ladies refused, so he twisted the bench with them still on it upsetting them and he took it.

Mom went and told our dad about it. This made him mad and the fight was on. It sounds like it became a free for all, men and women in the melee. They didn't look as dapper coming home as they did when they left. He carried one of the sleeves from his suit jacket that was ripped off at the seam most likely from one of the women, but he was uninjured except for a cut on his lip and bruises on his large hands which turn into powerful fists.

Our Aunt Delores, known as Doodie was getting married! Grandma Pierzina ordered chickens for the big day. Grandma, Weezie, Marie, Mom, Daddy and all six of us kids started catching, butchering, scalding, plucking, singeing (burns off any hair), and cleaning chickens. The farmer can tell when the chickens are still producing eggs and it would not be long before our flock reduced production and would be replaced with new chickens. It had been determined that the ones that were selected were no longer layers. As it turned out when we cleaned the chickens we found eggs inside a few chickens, some with just the membrane or very thin shell and some with their hard shells, which the chicken would have laid in the next day or so. We removed those with the hard shells and added them to the eggs that would be sold.

Cleaning chickens for a wedding

Grandma, Dwaine, Daddy, Weezie, (Marie's back), George, and Judy.
Putting the metal wash tub to good use—it was once our bath tub.

Almost done

Marie, Dwaine, Grandma, Dianne, Daddy, Weezie, Bette, George, Russell, and Judy.

We had just butchered and cleaned a lot of chickens when Doodie came to the farm to tell us that the wedding had been called off. She couldn't call because we didn't have a telephone. So what were we to do with all these chickens that were all cleaned when the wedding was called off? We canned them. There were no tin cans then, we used glass canning jars. Some larger jars had wider openings and with a little work a whole chicken would fit in. Then a flat rubber ring was placed on top of the opening and a lid placed on top of that which sealed the contents inside. The jars were then put in a pressure cooker and that long slow process cooked the chickens. This made it air tight, so very rarely was there any spoilage. To break the seal, you simply pulled on the rubber ring with a pair of pliers and used the ring again.

Dwaine remembers that he and Daddy were working in the yard and they noticed a car at the end of the driveway and someone got out and started walking toward them, but it was a long driveway so it took a while to make out who it was except for the fact that he wore an Army uniform. Daddy said, "I think that's my brother," and started walking toward him. Then he said, "It is my brother!" and started running to him. Dwaine said it was such a wonderful sight to see because they were so happy and big bear hugs going around. It was Uncle George and he must have hitched a ride out to the farm because whoever was driving the car drove off.

Our dad had a real healthy respect for Mother Nature. He'd been through and seen some of her devastation first hand. When he was eight years old a cyclone ripped through the town of Bowlus where he lived, striking his grandfather, John Pierzina's hotel which was about two blocks from his home, so it was very close.

Newspaper quote:

"When it reached the village it suddenly dropped several spirals, one which hit the New Grand Hotel and in an instant the flat roof was soaring in the air above the cornice, like the wings of a giant airship. The balance of the roof settled in the street filling it completely." And also this article, "George Pierzina had just

boarded up the walls of his new feed mill that day. They came down flat."

Barn down!

What's left of the Blair Farm barn.

When he was fifteen years old and living on the Blair farm, another storm came through with this Newspaper quote:

"The storm centered in Swan River, where the barn of Peter Blair was reduced to wreckage. What is believed to be a small twister centered on the 66x34 ft. building reducing it virtually to kindling wood. The silo adjacent to the barn was moved off its foundation but remained upright being well anchored. One window in the Blair house was smashed."

Our dad would describe how loud and horrible this storm was and like everybody that has been through it, it sounded like a freight train coming through.

One can well imagine when there was a storm brewing outside, we all had to head for the basement and stay there until it was over. There was no furniture or chairs to sit on, so we sat around on pieces of chopped wood from the wood pile or on the steps or even the dirt floor. It was very loud listening to the rolling thunder as it snapped and cracked, then lightening lit up the whole area. It stayed pretty dark down there except when the lightening flashed but we weren't afraid because our dad was with us. Mom always wanted to watch the storm so she never came down unless it got real treacherous. He always thought she was so foolish. On the roof of the house were lightning rods, made of pretty colored glass that would attract the lightning should it strike nearby and ground it safely. There were lightning rods on the barn too but not the other buildings.

One day on a hot day we were playing in the house when the sky got dark and ominous. Our dad was not at home, and we looked out the window and saw the biggest hailstones we'd ever seen. We ran outside laughing and having such a good time and thought this was just wonderful. It was incredible, the rain that came down was as warm as a warm shower but it was also loaded with the huge hail stones. Those big chunks of ice beating down on us, some of them were an inch and more in length. It didn't last long, five to maybe ten minutes if even that. Our dad returned home shortly after that and he just stood there in the yard overlooking his wheat field and cried. His beautiful wheat crop was lying flat on the ground, completely ruined. It was ready for cutting within the week and it was all gone. I've never seen him cry before and it was imprinted on me how for one person and event can be so enjoyable and for another it can be so devastating. I've never seen hail again that I don't remember that day but have never seen a day like that again either.

Sometimes our dad played poker, mostly with family, rarely drank, and he didn't smoke. He found that a candy bar tasted much better. I remember overhearing a conversation he was having with a self-righteous neighbor who was demeaning people who gambled. My dad said, "How can you look down on someone who gambles. What do you think farming is? Every year, it's a gamble if we're going to bring in a crop, if the chickens or the animals aren't going to get a disease. We gamble that the weather is going to be favorable, that we get enough rain, that it doesn't rain too much, and that the insects aren't going to eat up the crop. Every single farmer you know is the biggest gambler of all."

He also had a pretty good sense of humor. One year while filing his income taxes, there's an entry for 'Debts Owed.' He filled it in with 'Uncle Willie–a punch in the nose'. This was sent in to the Internal Revenue Service. In those days, you didn't make photocopies but instead sent in the original log book. He received it back from IRS but there was no notation or response to this entry but perhaps someone at that end got a chuckle out of it.

We weren't allowed to light lamps or lanterns when we were young and of course we couldn't turn on a switch for lights. We still didn't have electricity. One evening it was going from dusk to dark and Mom wasn't home. When our dad came into the house he had to light the lamp. He was filling the lamp with kerosene when some of it spilled over onto the new oilcloth that was on the kitchen table. When he struck the match, the whole top of the table caught fire. It was awfully scary for a while but he got it out without losing anything but the new oilcloth.

About 1949 we came into the modern world. We got electricity! That was quite a change for us. Dale Nelson says that our dad spearheaded getting electricity to the whole area. Before that none of our neighbors had it and when we got it, everybody else did too. All new poles and wires had to be stung for miles.

Our new kitchen

Only known picture of the inside of the house except for the earlier picture of Dianne and Judy.

Every building we owned was wired. We had a tall yard light installed in the center of the yard and it lit up the whole yard from the house to the barn. We no longer had to carry a lantern to go out to the barn or chicken house. When the moon was bright we could see alright but once you entered the building you needed a light. The pantry was converted to a real bathroom. We didn't need the pantry anymore because in the kitchen were new cupboards and sink, no more dish pans and no more pump, we had running water from a real faucet. Our wood burning cook stove was traded in for an electric stove, our smoke-belching washing machine was traded in but for another wringer washer, and we got a refrigerator. Life was good.

Not only did we get electricity but around that same time, we got a telephone too; and again, so did all the other farms in the area. Dale didn't know if our dad was responsible for that, too, but if one were to hazard a guess, he most likely was. Our phone number was 26-W-2. There were no private lines, so we shared our phone line with five of the neighbors. The numbers ranged from 26-W-1 to 26-W-6, meaning that the last number was the number of rings that went to each house. Ours was two rings, represented by the last number in our phone number. If the neighbor who had six numbers didn't answer their phone, it rang and rang in our house, too, and could get pretty maddening at times. Aunt Ruby's number was 10-F-21 but it didn't ring 21 times.

To make a call, we had to ring the operator which was a crank handle on the side of the phone box. This brought the operator on the line and you told her what number you were calling and she plugged you into their line. If you wanted to call a neighbor who was on our same set of numbers, you had to ring for the operator tell her the number, then you had to hang up the phone and listen to the rings and when it stopped ringing then you could be pretty certain that they picked up their phone. If they hung up thinking there was nobody on the line, then you had to go through the whole process again until they were on the line and you were able to connect. Sometimes a neighbor picked up the receiver just to listen to the conversation.

One day we were having a storm and Mom was sitting on a chair under the wall mounted phone. Suddenly a big ball of fire came from the mouthpiece and was visible half-way across the kitchen. I don't remember if it damaged the telephone or not.

A real treat was going to the movies which we did about every other month if the movie was appropriate. We usually went to the theater in Randall, where admission was nine cents, while the Little Falls Theater cost fourteen cents. Grandpa Hankes worked at Camp Ripley and was able to get us into camp for a current movie that was being shown to the soldiers. There was no admission charge for those movies. Generally we only saw Western films. Our heroes all wore white hats; Tex Ritter, Gene Autry, and best of all, Roy Rogers. We also saw movies such as "The Yearling," or Walt Disney features. We loved 'Song of the South" with Uncle Remus.

We did see a movie that was normally off limits for us, it was called, "The Thing." It was about a large man that had been frozen for an eon, and then thawed out and he came back to life. The setting of the movie was in Alaska, where there was lots of snow on the ground and they were isolated. Then we returned to our home which has the same setting as the movie. There was lots of snow on the ground and we too were isolated. We hadn't learned to differentiate between movies and real life. There were six kids who never got decent night's sleep after that. Going down into that spooky basement became absolute torture because every one of us knew that monster man—that now had a face—had found his way to our basement, our barn, our silo, our chicken house, or our outhouse, which we still used when baths were taken. We saw the movie in winter, a few months before moving to California, which may account for each of us reaching adulthood. Had we stayed on the farm we each would have died of fright.

When our dad was a small boy about ten years old, he fell through the ice on the Bowlus River. He was pulled to safety by his brothers and sisters and put on a sled and taken home, but was like an ice cube when they got there. From that time, he had trouble with his breathing and sometimes had arthritis problems in the winter; the basis was believed to have been caused from the fall in the icy water.

In the fall of 1950, he went into the hospital for quite some time because his arthritis was so bad. When he came home, he could only sit in front of the stove wrapped in a blanket. This was difficult for him because he was such a hardworking man. Dwaine and Mom did the bulk of the work while he was laid up, although we all took on extra chores.

To add to the income, Mom got a job in Little Falls. One day she caught the school bus with us and the driver dropped her off at Munsingwear, a garment factory and she had a job that same day. Her income of $25 per week supported us through the winter. She held down her job and with Dwaine, they kept the farm going while Daddy was in the hospital and after he came home.

Dr. Fortier told our dad that if he continued to live in Minnesota, he could count on becoming a complete cripple and recommended that he move to a warmer climate. The following fall of 1951, he went to California where his brothers Howard and George lived. He went by train and while going over a mountain pass they hit a snow storm. The men had to get off the train and clear the tracks with shovels so the train could go through. He spent the whole winter with his brothers. At that time, he and his brother George Blair became partners when they formed an earth moving construction company. They called it Bay Excavators.

Our dad returned home and it was time to plan for an auction. The date was set for March 24, 1952 but if the weather was unfavorable, it would be postponed for a week. That's just what happened, and that was announced over the local radio station; it had been raining for the past week. It continued to rain through the next week and the dirt road to our farm was quite impassable but the auction couldn't be postponed again. Turnout was disappointing but all true friends attended. The road was full of deep ruts and many vehicles had to be pulled out. Some farmers were smart enough to bring the team of horses and wagon. It was an exciting day for us and although it continued to rain all day, that didn't put a damper on our excitement. The lunch wagon gave us all the food we wanted. We didn't know they were putting in on a tab for our parents to pay, we thought it was all free. Many items didn't go as high as was hoped, so some of the machinery was bought back by our dad, which he sold later for a better price.

Auction Paper

Living on a farm is not an easy life. You worked from sun-up to sundown and tried to complete all the jobs that needed to get done with what daylight there was. Farming is also a hazardous occupation. Everybody knows of a neighboring farmer who was maimed and injured on their farms. Missing fingers from the machinery was the most common. There were no weekends off to go visiting. There is no such thing as a holiday. Christmas was treated as any other day of the week. The cows needed to be milked and the chickens fed. We were always the last to arrive at a gathering, and the first to leave. As a child, I decided that I would never marry a farmer. I found the idea of moving to California very exciting. I was also a few years' older now and finding boys a little interesting. Far more interesting than being chased by a bull.

We left Minnesota on April 11, 1952, the day after Easter. All our belongings were in a recently purchased used panel truck with the name Schinabarger Plumbing and Heating written on the side. We also bought a new 1952 Chevrolet sedan, which Mom drove. We spent our last night at Grandma Pierzina's house and during the night, she decided to make the trip with us.

Traveling the long roads we soon became familiar with the Burma Shave signs that were posted on fence posts. Each post had one line and we couldn't wait to see what the next line was going to read. Because we had never seen them before, they gave us a great deal of joy along the way.

Around the curve

Lickety-split

Beautiful car

Wasn't it

The roads were winding and curving and mostly two lane roads with construction in every state. Our dad stopped at every Historical Marker from Minnesota to California. We each had to get out of the car and read every one of them and there must have been 500; many of them about Louis and Clark. He said, "You will never pass this way again and this will be your only chance to see it." He was right; the crooked roads have all been straightened and replaced with freeways. Grandma prayed every mile of the way, especially on the mountain roads where there were canyons below and curves ahead; we would hear "Jesus, Mary, and Joseph be with us on our way".

We left the cold weather, the barren trees and arrived in El Sobrante, California where our dad had purchased a new three bedroom home before he returned back to Minnesota. Our new home was a very good choice because it was a semi-country location where there were open fields all around us with horses and cows on the hillsides. The sun was shining and it was warm. To our surprise everything was green with flowers and roses blooming everywhere. None of us kids had ever been more than a few miles from our farm, so we were shocked at what we saw. A whole new way of life has now been placed in front of us and new paths to follow.

Last day as Minnesota residents

Picture taken at Grandma Pierzina's.
Back: Dwaine, Mom, Daddy.
Front: Bette, Dianne, Judy, Russell, and George.

Heading out

Dwaine, George, Russell, Dianne, Judy and Daddy got a dusting of snow during the night.

Badlands of South Dakota

Dwaine, Bette, Russell, George, and Mom.

Dwaine, Dianne, Mom, Russell, and George

Grandma, Bette, and Judy on other side of panel truck.

Taking a lunch break

Dianne, Grandma, Mom, Judy, Bette, Dwaine, George, Russell (on right).

Russell, George, and Bette

Panel truck drew a lot of attention on trip
Many of them seemed to know where Long Prairie was.

Too many people for one motel—needed two of them

Dianne, Daddy, Grandma, Dwaine, Judy. Bette (in panel, she was
navigator, reading the map for trip).

Dwaine Pierzina
1952, 16 Years Old

Bette Pierzina
1952, 14 Years Old

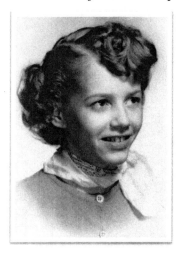

Dianne Pierzina
1952, 12 Years Old

Judy Pierzina
1952, 11 Years Old

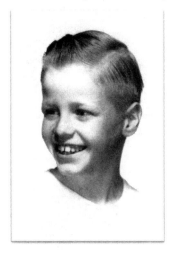

Russell Pierzina
1952, 9 Years Old

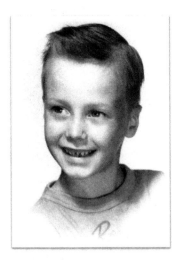

George Pierzina
1952, 7 Years Old

Our Dad

"Daddy's Hands"

I remember Daddy's hands, folded silently in prayer.

And reaching out to hold me, when I had a nightmare.

You could read quite a story, in the calluses and lines.

Years of work and worry had left their mark behind.

I remember Daddy's hands, how they held my Mama tight,

And patted my back, for something done right.

There are things that I've forgotten, that I loved about the man,

But I'll always remember the love in Daddy's hands.

Daddy's hands were soft and kind when I was cryn'.

Daddy's hands were hard as steel when I'd done wrong.

Daddy's hands weren't always gentle,

Tales of Our Youth: Generations of Love & Hope ~ Elizabeth Brown

But I've come to understand.

There was always love in Daddy's hands.

I remember Daddy's hands, working 'til they bled.

Sacrificed unselfishly just to keep us all fed.

If I could do things over, I'd live my life again.

And never take for granted the love in Daddy's hands

~ Holly Dunn

1955

Our mother, Helen and our dad, Alois

Ella Robinson & Frank Hankes

October 23, 1911–St. Cloud, MN

Frank & Ella Hankes

50th Anniversary 1961
They were married for 70 years

Frank Hankes Family

Frank Jr. (known as Boy), Helen (known as Girlie), Della, Orlo, Ruby, Ella and Frank.

*Missing is their son Elmer who drown at 19 years of age.

George Pierzina and Louise Blair

May 10, 1910
Sobieski, MN

A portion of George's implement shop

George on left.

George and Louise Pierzina's Children

Back: Howard, Florence (known as Flossie), George,
Russell, Delores (known as Doodie).
Front: Clarence and Ione (holding Alois's picture)
Both mother Louise and Alois died in 1974.

Note: Howard, George, and Russell changed their names to
Blair.

Louise Blair Pierzina

❧ *Epilogue* ❦

The farm was sold to a family who defaulted on the loan and about three years later, the farm was repossessed. The first winter they owned the farm, they put their chickens in the upstairs quarters of the house. Our bedroom!!! It's beyond belief that anyone could live like that. The house was destroyed and had to be torn down. It was unsalvageable after they were through with it. As for the chicken house, they cut a hole out of one of the side walls and made it a garage or shop of some sort. Before leaving the premises they retaliated by knocking all the windows and casing out of the barn and did a lot of damage. Dale Nelson bought the farm. He repaired all the buildings and owns it yet today. He never lived there; he stayed on his own family farm. Our family has been so grateful to Dale and his wife Joanne for buying it and they have always made it available to us anytime any of us are in Minnesota visiting and for many years that was very important. Our roots were so deep into that farm. Dale says that he has had many offers for the farm but he wouldn't sell it. He says he loves that farm; it has many happy memories for him.

After moving to California, Mom and Daddy's marriage dissolved and they were divorced about 1960, after the four oldest children were married. She was married and full of responsibilities at such a young age, perhaps she felt that life passed her by. They tried to reconcile, but it didn't work. They did, however, continue to love each other for the rest of their lives. Into his final days he still said that she was the finest woman he ever met and into her final days, she had their wedding picture on the wall where it was always in her view. Dianne took it down one time—but not for long.

Mom moved back to Minnesota and eventually remarried Orvil Karlstad. Our dad never remarried but continued with his construction business and it thrived. All of his sons and son-in-laws were employed by Bay Excavators.

About 1960, our dad developed a rash that plagued him for the rest of his life. He spent many weeks in San Francisco hospitals where doctors worldwide checked him out, but no answer could be found as to the cause. The only treatment that would control it, but not cure it, was a shot of Cortisone which had many bad side effects. He suffered a stroke in 1972 which was disabling, but not paralyzing. Our saddest loss of all was on December 21, 1974 when he died of a heart attack. The Cortisone he'd been taking for so many years surely cut his life short. All six of his children and most of his sisters and brothers were with him at Doctor's Hospital in Pinole when we were ushered into another room. The day was dreary and pouring down rain beating against the windows as we sat in the waiting room, dreading the worst. Suddenly there were hundreds of birds singing outside in the drenching rain. They sang their hearts—out then, just as suddenly, all was silent. We all looked at each other and we knew; God and the heavens had welcomed him.

Mom and Orvil lived in Minneapolis where he was a baker. They bought the home that her father built and moved there in 1980. She continued with her wonderful art of cooking and welcomed all who popped in, and no matter what the hour was they got something to eat. Dianne moved in with them and turned their yard into a beautiful park setting that they enjoyed every day. Orvil died in 1997. When Mom was about eighty-one years old, she slipped and fell on the ice and broke the ball in her shoulder from which she never fully recovered. That ended her baking bread because she could no longer kneed the bread dough and she also could no longer shoot her gun. She went downhill at a slow pace from that time under the watchful eye of Dianne who took wonderful care of her. She died in her home on August 16, 2007.

Our little brother Georgie Porgie was such a unique special person. He had a little Einstein brain which was always working inventing something new. Always inventing but never interested in getting rich. He was content with his surroundings and little worry about tomorrow. He had a broken tooth which he didn't take care of and that resulted in cancer of the tongue. He died in his home in El Sobrante, CA on July 23, 2009—he was sixty-four years old.

The End

For now...

"See Me"

What do you see, nurses, what do you see?

What are you thinking when you're looking at me?

Crabby old woman, not very wise,

Uncertain of habit, with faraway eyes?

Who dribbles her food and makes no reply

When you say in a loud voice, 'I do wish you'd try!"

Who seems not to notice the things that you do,

And forever is losing a stocking or shoe

Who, resisting or not, lets you do as you will,

With bathing and feeding, the long day to fill

Is that what you're thinking? Is that what you see?

Then open your eyes; you're not looking at me.

I'll tell you who I am as I sit here so still,

As I do at your bidding, as I eat at your will.

I'm a small child of ten...with a father and mother,

Brothers and sisters, who love one another.

A young girl of sixteen, with wings on her feet,

Dreaming that soon now a lover she'll meet.

A bride soon at twenty—my heart gives a leap,

Remembering the vows that I promised to keep.

At twenty-five now, I have young of my own,

Who need me to guide and a secure happy home.

A woman of thirty, my young now grown fast,

Tales of Our Youth: Generations of Love & Hope ~ Elizabeth Brown

Bound to each other with ties that should last.

At forty, my young sons have grown and are gone,

But my man's beside me to see I don't mourn.

At fifty once more, babies play 'round my knee,

Again we know children, my loved one and me.

Dark days are upon me, my husband is dead.

I look at the future, I shudder with dread.

For my young are all rearing young of their own,

And I think of the years and the love that I've known.

I'm now an old woman...and nature is cruel;

'Tis jest to make old age look like a fool.

The body, it crumbles, grace and vigor depart,

There is now a stone where I once had a heart.

But inside this old carcass a young girl still dwells,

And now and again my battered heart swells.

I remember the joys, I remember the pain,

And I'm loving and living life over again.

I think of the years...all too few, gone too fast,

And accept the stark fact that nothing can last.

So open your eyes people, open and see,

Not a crabby old woman; look closer...see ME!!

~ Unknown author

❧ About Elizabeth Brown ❦

I read the poem "See Me" and I wanted my grandchildren to know that there was more to me than a crabby old woman, so I decided to write about when we were children.

I've always enjoyed writing but never took it seriously. Mostly writing about events that happened and letters

This will give you a glimpse into a way of life that you would never have imagined and to give you a better understanding of what life can be like living on a farm. There have been many inventions and improvements since these days of past. Plastic, tin, foil, or hair sprays are just a few of the items that had not been invented yet, much less microwave ovens, televisions, and computers.

Life was wonderful for the most part. The sky was the bluest, the clouds were the whitest, and the rain in the summer time was the warmest and smelled the freshest. There was an assortment of smells of the barn, the pigs in the pigpen, the chickens with their egg and feather odors, and the wonderful smell of freshly mown hay. Wild flowers grew all around us and plenty of wild berries to be picked. We were only limited by our imaginations and in our case, imaginations ran wild. What one didn't think of, one of the other five did.

We were insatiably curious. Always present was the question, 'I wonder what would happen if...' and we had to find out. Living on the farm gave us all a vast knowledge base to draw from for the rest of our lives.

We're all very grateful and glad to have shared our lives with each other and with our parents. Each and every one was a unique individual person. Our years on the farm are forever etched in our minds and in our hearts and have become the fabric of our being. It was truly a time of innocence.

After we left the farm, I know I had the best of both worlds, being raised on the farm and then I adapted quickly to living my teen years in an urban setting.

I was a stay-at-home mom raising four children while our family enjoyed all the outdoor activities, mainly boating and water skiing. After twenty-seven years of marriage I became a widow and had to find a way to support myself. I enrolled as a full-time student in the same school I graduated from years before learning all the computer programs that were offered. I worked as a temp for several years, unable to tie myself down to a single job always needing the freedom to change course if I wanted.

Throughout the years, I was fortunate enough to pursue any project that interested me. Early on, my best friend was my sewing machine and between us we were able to create just about everything including wedding dresses. I became interested in needlepoint, creating unusual pieces where I replaced the thread with beads. I mastered stained glass and oil painting. I've amassed a huge amount of genealogy. I needed to get my old family movie films transferred but couldn't get the quality work I wanted done, so I went to school at the local college and learned Final Cut. If you are familiar with Final Cut, it is a challenging program, especially for a grandmother.

I do feel that I have been blessed with many talents and have put all of them to good use. Just as when we were kids, a thought comes in my head, "I wonder what would happen if..." and I always had the chance to explore and create.

The following by Erma Bombeck says it well for me: "When I stand before God at the end of my life, I would hope that I would not have a single bit of talent left, and could say, 'I used everything you gave me.'"